Remembering Melanie

Heartlines

Books by Jill Young
Three Summers On
Just Matty's Luck
Valentine Night

Books by Pam Lyons
Latchkey Girl
Ms Perfect
One Of The Boys
Wish You Were Here
Girl Overboard

Books by Anita Eires
Californian Summer
If Only...
Teacher's Pet

Books by Mary Hooper
Love Emma XXX
Opposites Attract
Remembering Melanie

Books by Barbara Jacobs
Two Times Two

Books by Anita Davies
Always In My Dreams

Books by Vicki Tyler
Danny And The Real Me

Books by Ann De Gale
Island Encounter

Books by Anthea Cohen
Dangerous Love
Substance And Shadow

Books by David S. Williams
Give Me Back My Pride
Forgive And Forget
No Time For Regrets

Books by Ann Ruffell
Friends For Keeps
Leaving Home
Baby Face
No Place To Hide
Drumbeat

Books by Lorna Read
Images
The Name is 'Zero'
On Wheels Of Love

Books by Jane Butterworth
Spotlight On Sam
Wild In The Country

Books by John Harvey
Wild Love

Books by Jane Pitt
Autumn Always Comes
Stony Limits
Rainbows For Sale
Headlines

Books by Margaret West
Search For A Stranger
Home Before Dark
Date With Danger

heartlines

Mary Hooper
Remembering Melanie

A Pan Original

First published 1989 by Pan Books Ltd,
Cavaye Place, London SW10 9PG
9 8 7 6 5 4 3 2 1
© Mary Hooper
ISBN 0 330 30596 4
Typesetting by Input Typesetting Ltd, London, SW19
Printed and bound in Great Britain by
Richard Clay Ltd, Bungay, Suffolk

This book is sold subject to the condition that it
shall not, by way of trade or otherwise, be lent, re-sold,
hired out, or otherwise circulated without the publisher's prior
consent in any form of binding or cover other than that in which
it is published and without a similar condition including this
condition being imposed on the subsequent purchaser

Chapter 1

I can't remember the first time I saw Jacko at the bus stop ... September, I suppose, when the new term started, but I can remember clearly the first time we spoke – and the date, because it was Melanie's birthday and the day I began wanting to know exactly what had happened to her.

The morning had started off pretty much as usual: there was the steady drone of my father's voice from downstairs while I got ready, then his call: 'Goodbye, Joanna,' followed by the ritual handing over of the umbrella in the hall and the kiss on Mum's cheek.

I did my hair and came down then. I always hang about upstairs until my father's gone; he's so slow and ponderous in the mornings, it really gets on my nerves. Everything has to be in its right place: his own particular knife next to his own particular plate, the toast at the right temperature, the coffee just the right shade of brown – and God help the whole house if the morning paper's late.

I really didn't notice then that Mum was quieter than usual. She is always quiet in the mornings, fetching and carrying for Dad, quietly attending to his every wish. There's not much equality for women in *our* house. Mum is small and round and old-fashioned, with a tight perm and not the slightest idea about clothes. Her lack of style, unfortunately, has been passed on to me. I can never decide what looks best with what.

I ate my cereal, cleaned my teeth and started off for the bus stop. All as usual. It was just starting to drizzle with rain and Mum's cry of 'Don't you think you should wear your rainhat, dear?' floated down the path behind me.

I waved and frowned at her. 'I'll be OK,' I said, and she went in again. Rainhat! She'd bought me an awful Sou'wester thing at the weekend, one of those with a turned up brim all the way round, and I looked just like a fisherman in it. My school uniform is pretty horrific anyway: muddy brown A-line skirt and white blouse with a canary yellow jumper. On top of this, in the winter, we have to wear cloaks, great billowy things that have the young kids calling out 'Hey, Batman!' to us. As I said, I'm not at all trendy, but I really drew the line at looking like a fisherman, especially as I knew that I might be seeing the boy at the bus stop. He was still just 'the boy' then, he didn't have a name.

He was there before me. We smiled, as we always did, and then I stood about six people behind him and looked at the back of his head, wondering if he could feel me staring. He was usually at the bus stop before me so I'd got to know the back of him quite well. He had very straight blond hair, short at the front and quite long at the back, and when he turned sideways, a straight nose and a slightly furrowed expression. I'd never got close enough to see the colour of his eyes but I'd guessed they were blue.

I didn't know much about him then: only that he looked nice and he went to the Greatlands, the sixth-form college in the next town. I knew that he didn't go to the boys' school that matches my all-girls' school, because he didn't wear the uniform. He usually wore jeans and trainers, and a bright blue skiing jacket with green flashes down the front.

It kept on drizzling; the bus was late and when it came along, massively crowded, everyone swarmed to get on. I didn't swarm, I just stood where I was and let everyone fight each other for places. When everyone had got on and the bus had left with people still hanging from the platform and arguing with each other, to my surprise there was just him and me and a stout business man left standing there.

'I couldn't face it, could you?' he said to me. 'It doesn't matter if I'm in later today, anyway.'

I smiled at him uncertainly. He wasn't the first boy I'd spoken to or anything like that, but he was the first *proper* boy, if you know what I mean: the first boy I'd seen and liked and thought a lot about.

'You have to be in at quarter to, do you?' he said cheerfully, not seeming to notice that I'd been struck dumb. 'I suppose from your get-up you must go to Northcote.'

I shrugged my cloak round me and pulled a face. 'It's awful, isn't it? I get called "Batman" all the time!'

He smiled. He had brown eyes, which surprised me; when I thought about him later, I'd have to revise my day-dreams. 'I don't think you look like Batman,' he said. 'I think you look rather mysterious. Like the French Lieutenant's Woman or someone.'

'We're doing that for 'A Level!' I said.

'So are we!'

We discussed what other English books we were doing and what exams we were taking, and when the next bus came along we just naturally got on it together and sat downstairs at the front. He was very easy to talk to; easier than some of the girls at school, actually. I hadn't thought that talking to a boy you really liked would be as easy as that. I thought there would be long silences and that you'd have to have swotted up beforehand on football and motorbikes to make sure you had enough to talk about.

He asked my name and I told him it was Joanna.

'But only my father calls me that – everyone else calls me Jo.'

'My name . . . wait for this . . . is Michael Jackson!' he said. 'OK, you can mob me now.'

For a moment I couldn't think what he was talking about.

'Michael Jackson!' he repeated, then he turned his head and stared at me in amazement. 'Don't tell me you've never heard of Michael Jackson!' he said incredulously.

I caught on. 'The singer! Oh, of course I have.'

'Only just, though,' he said.

'Well. . .' There didn't seem to be any harm in telling him. 'It's my father, you see. He doesn't let me have Top of the Pops or anything like that on so I don't exactly think in terms of pop singers.'

His jaw dropped. 'Why doesn't he?'

I shrugged. 'He thinks pop music is corrupting. And he doesn't like me watching too much TV – says it interferes with my homework.'

He was still looking at me with an amazed expression.

'He must be out of the ark!'

I laughed. 'He *is* pretty old. They both are.'

'So you never . . . not even the odd chart show?'

'Oh, sometimes when he's out I get to see one of the early shows. I'm usually pretty busy, though; often I don't bother.'

'Crumbs,' he said.

The bus lurched and swayed so that our bodies leaned against each other.

'I thought you looked kind of different,' he said thoughtfully, 'and it's not just your get-up. When I first saw you at the bus stop you just didn't look like anyone else – the girls at college, for instance.'

I was pleased he'd noticed me, thought about me, but when he mentioned the girls at college I felt a twinge of something I later realized was jealousy. They were probably all really glamorous: blonde streaked hair and make-up and short skirts. Some hopes for me, then. With Mum and Dad the way they were I wouldn't be allowed to look like that even when I'd *left* school.

The bus stopped; he nudged me. 'This is you, isn't it?' he said, and I realized with a start that it was my stop. 'See you, Jo!' he said as I got up all in a flurry.

'Goodbye . . . Michael – Mike?' I said.

He laughed and half-turned as I pushed my way off. 'It's Jacko!' I heard him saying, 'everyone calls me Jacko.'

Michael Jackson . . . Jacko . . . I said over and over to myself as I walked through the school gates. I knew him now. I'd spoken to him, sat next to him, knew his name!

Jacko . . . Jacko. OK, I didn't for one moment think anything would come of it – I mean, I wasn't pretending to myself that it would lead to a proper date or anything, it was just enough to know him as a person. Dates were what some of the girls at school had: the ones who took in their A-line skirts so they were tight, had boyfriends called Kevin and Justin and went to discos.

As I walked across the car park I heard someone yell my name.

'I saw you!' Sara shouted in a found-you-out sort of voice. 'I saw you on the bus!'

I turned and she hurried over to catch me up. I didn't much like Sara; she was one of the bright and beautiful ones, the disco-goers. She was brittle and sarcastic, always wanting to know things about you and, when she knew them, passing them on, giggling about them.

'You're a dark horse, I must say,' she said. 'I saw you chatting to Jacko nineteen to the dozen. Nearly forgot your stop, didn't you?'

'Mm.' I was embarrassed – and annoyed that she knew him. I'd wanted to keep him private and special. I began walking faster. 'We're late, aren't we?'

'Never mind that! Why are you always in a hurry to get into class. Proper swot, aren't you?'

We went through the swing doors into school and Sara undid her cloak and tossed her hair back.

'This rain!' she said, running a hand through it like a comb. 'It makes my hair absolutely frightful!' It looked wonderful, actually: because it was wet it had gone into a mass of fine curls and waves which haloed round her head in a blonde cloud. I started to go off to my tutor group, but she caught my arm.

'Just a sec,' she said. 'How long have you known Jacko?'

'Not long,' I said. 'I hardly know him, anyway. We just ... just chat a bit, that's all.' I didn't want to tell her that this was the first morning we'd spoken.

'That's what you tell me!' she said. 'You quiet ones are the worst. We have to watch out for you.'

'I don't know what you mean,' I said, because I didn't.

'I don't know what you mean!' she gibed, imitating my voice. 'I bet you don't. Little Miss Goody-Two-Shoes, aren't you?'

'I don't know what...' I began again, uncomfortably. Sara almost scared me; she was so dazzling, so scathing and so confident about everything.

'Jo!' I turned in relief as Nicki, one of the girls in my tutor group, came down the corridor. 'Miss Turner's looking for you.'

'Right!' I said. 'I'd better go.' Miss Turner was our group tutor and she usually relied on me to distribute letters or put notices on boards.

'Run then: run rabbit, run!' Sara said. 'Don't keep Miss Turner waiting, whatever you do!'

I went, pink in the face, unable to think of a reply and glad to get away. Sara had always picked on me, ever since the third year when we'd all sort of distributed ourselves into the Beauties and ... well, the rabbits. The Beauties had their followers, the girls who weren't quite beautiful enough to be included in the real 'in' crowd but were just honorary members, and they hung around the Beauties, grateful to have their clothes borrowed, to be included in trips to the disco and occasionally fixed up with blind dates. The rabbits were left to their own devices. Because I didn't hang around the Beauties and I was even more of a grey rabbit than most – my father had seen to that – Sara treated me like a real oddball.

I saw Nicki again in the canteen at lunchtime. The

sixth form had their own eating area, but we had to go over to the main canteen to get our food, then bring it back to our block.

'Was Sara having a go at you?' she asked as we stood in the sandwich queue.

I nodded. 'She saw me talking to this boy she knows on the bus and I don't think she liked it.' I'd been wondering all morning how well Sara knew him; whether he'd told her she looked like the French Lieutenant's Woman, too...

'You want to stand up to her, you know. Don't let her pick on you.'

I looked at Nicki. She was a Beauty, but she was better than most of them. She wasn't one of the gritty, sarcastic ones. 'It's all right for you,' I said. 'I never know what to say.'

'Just tell her to shut up. Easy!'

I reached for a sandwich. 'It's OK,' I shrugged. 'It doesn't bother me.'

'Well, it ought to,' she said. 'She shouldn't be allowed to get away with it. It's bullying. If we were in the first year and she was picking on someone...'

'It doesn't matter,' I said. 'It goes right over my head most of the time.' We paid for our sandwiches, then walked back to the sixth-form block together.

'Who is this guy, anyway? Is he nice?'

I nodded. 'Very nice.' But I didn't want to talk about him; not even to Nicki.

'Are you going out with him?'

'No. I've only just started chatting to him today.'

'Will you go out with him? If he asks?'

I was silent, thinking. I still couldn't imagine me on a date, though. Not a proper date. 'I don't know,'

I said. 'I wouldn't know what to do. I don't suppose he'll ask me, anyway.'

'Jo,' Nicki said to me suddenly. 'You shouldn't put yourself down, you know. You could really be attractive. I mean, you *are* attractive, you're just a bit ... well, old-fashioned. If you did something about your hair ... and d'you ever wear *any* make-up?'

I shook my head. I had make-up, of course. I'd messed about with some eyeshadow once, though, and my father had shouted at me that I looked like a tart, so I'd never worn it since.

'You ought to. You've got lovely eyes – you could just wear mascara and they'd look huge. And why don't you get someone to style your hair? It's lovely and long but it just sort of *hangs* there, doesn't it?'

I laughed. Nicki was trying her hardest to tell me nicely that I was a frump. My hairstyle: well, as she said, it's long and straight but just hangs there. Mum has a woman who comes to the house to do hers, and she's always done mine as well: half an inch off every so often for the split ends, fringe cut to just above the eyebrows. Dead boring, but then I'd never really bothered about my appearance. Why should I, when I never went anywhere?

'I bet if you were to change your image a bit, this boy ... what's his name?'

'Jacko.'

'This Jacko would fancy you like mad. You ought to try it. I'd like to see Sara's nose put out of joint.'

I unwrapped my sandwiches. 'It's OK,' I said. 'Thanks for making the effort and all that, but he's not going to ask me out. He only spoke to me today because we happened to be on our own at the bus stop.'

'Oh, go on!' she said. 'Just good friends, are you?'

'Not even that,' I said.

Well, it was daft to think anything could come of it. Rabbits didn't have dates.

Chapter 2

It was very quiet when I got home. Mum sometimes worked afternoons at the Oxfam shop, so for a while I thought no one was in.

I let myself into the hall and stood there for a while in the dim light, sniffing the musty, polishy smell. Our house wasn't like the houses of the girls at school: I knew that, even though I wasn't a frequent visitor of other people's houses. Our house was old-fashioned, with great lumps of oak furniture, lino on the floor and little mats placed here and there for you to skid on. The paintwork was just as it was when we'd moved in: brown and cream, and the kitchen had crummy old units with sliding glass doors that rattled and stuck when you tried to slide them along.

I'd been amazed when I first went to someone else's house: the paintwork was white, the furniture was some sort of light wood and the curtains were a bright colour; it had been like stepping into a magazine home. It was only later that I realized that most houses were like that – it was ours that was the odd one out.

I hung my cloak on a hook in the hall: we've got one of those ancient coat stands with four hooks, a tiny round mirror and a selection of clothes brushes hanging on it.

'I'm in!' I shouted, just in case Mum was home, though when she was she usually came into the hall to meet me and then we'd go into the kitchen together to have a cup of tea.

'In here, dear,' she called from the sitting room, and when I went in she was just sitting in front of the electric fire, staring at it.

'What's up?' I said. 'Aren't you well?'

She sighed. 'No, I'm fine. I just haven't felt like doing much today.'

I sat down on the settee. It was huge and flowered, and had those little mats along the back that you're supposed to rest your head on. I would have liked to have gone upstairs straight away and think about the day, think about Jacko, but I obviously had to find out what was up with Mum first.

'What . . . have you got a headache or something?' I asked.

Mum shook her head. 'It . . . well, it's Melanie's birthday, that's all.'

'Oh,' I said, and I tried to look sympathetic. I suppose I should have been used to Mum's Melanie days: days when she'd just sit around not doing much, just occasionally dabbing at her eyes. Melanie was my sister but I'd never known her. She'd died shortly after I was born, before we'd come to live in this house.

'You're getting so like her, dear,' Mum said now. 'Her colouring, her hair. . .'

I smiled uneasily. I didn't much like being compared to someone who was dead.

'If only. . .' Mum said with a catch in her voice, and then shook her head and sniffed again into her hanky.

'I'll make you a cup of tea,' I said quickly, and went into the kitchen. I hated Mum crying, especially when it was about Melanie. There was one thing, though, I knew she'd be OK by the time Dad came home; she always was. She never let Dad see her upset about Melanie.

I put the kettle on, thinking about Melanie. I'd never been all that curious about her, actually; it was all history, she didn't concern me. I'd just grown up knowing about her, and taking her life and death for granted. Sometimes, though, when my father was being absolutely impossible, I wondered what having an older sister would be like. Maybe he wouldn't be such a dictator if there had been someone else in the house, someone who might have stood up to him and not been such a rabbit. Maybe *she* would have been able to wear decent clothes, play records, have pop programmes on, go on dates. She might have been a Beauty – and she could have paved the way for me to be one, too.

Mum came wandering into the kitchen as I poured the hot water into the teapot. She looked as if she'd made an effort to pull herself together.

'I'll be all right now,' she said, smiling bravely. 'You won't tell your father that I've been moping, will you? He doesn't like it.'

'Of course I won't.' I got out some biscuits. 'You ought to get out a bit, Mum, it would stop you brooding about things. Why don't you get yourself a part-time job or something?'

She gave a hollow laugh. 'Your father would have a fit, that's why. He thinks I ought to be here at home looking after you two.'

'But I'm not a baby!' I said. 'I could quite easily let myself in and get my own tea. You don't have to be here for me anymore.'

She shook her head. 'I ought to be. In case. I had a job once before, you see, when Melanie was a teenager, and your father didn't approve. He blamed me, said it was my fault she was going around with boys and had gone off the rails.'

I had to smile. 'Gone off the rails? What d'you mean – that she had a boyfriend?'

'She was a popular girl...' Mum said, hardly seeming to hear me. 'Always had friends calling. Your father hated it. He likes the house to himself.'

I sipped my tea slowly. She *had* been one of the Beauties, then.

'How old was she when she died?' I asked Mum suddenly.

'What?'

'When she died ... how old was she?'

'Sixteen,' Mum said.

'So how old would she have been today?

'Thirty-two,' Mum said. 'A woman. She wouldn't be my child anymore.'

I drained my cup of tea; there was something puzzling me. 'Why haven't we got any photographs of her? Hasn't she got any things ... any clothes? Did you get rid of everything when she died?'

Mum was silent. 'We moved to this house when you were a baby,' she said after a long while, 'and we made a new start. We put the past behind us ... we wanted to go where no one knew us and knew what an unhappy time we'd had. We cleared Melanie's room and gave most of her things away.'

'But...' I was appalled. 'It's as if she's never been, then. You must have kept *something*.'

'There are some photographs of when she was little.'

'I've seen those in the album. What about later . . . when she was my age?'

Did she have to go to an all-girls school, I wondered, did she buy records, go to concerts, how did she have her hair? Was she very trendy? Suddenly I wanted to know about her.

'There are. . .' Mum stopped, faltered, 'there are some things of hers in a box in the loft: some of her special things I didn't have the heart to throw away. Your father doesn't know. I kept them because. . .'

'Because it's only natural that you should!' I said. 'Surely Dad would be able to see that.'

'I don't think so, dear. Your father has very set ideas.'

'You're telling me! You ought to stand up to him more.' I shook my head. 'We both should.'

A look shot across her face – a resolute look, as if she was quite pleased with herself. 'I stood up to him when I had to,' she said quietly.

'What d'you mean?'

But she didn't reply. 'She was a lovely girl,' was all she said. 'If only she was here today.'

It was my turn to be silent for a while, thinking. 'You've never told me exactly how she died,' I said after a moment.

'An accident,' Mum said.

'Yes, but what sort of accident? You've only said things like she's dead because she went off the rails . . . how did she really die, though?'

'I really don't. . .'

'I mean, was it a motorbike accident or a car – was one of her boyfriends drunk when he was driving or something?'

'Yes,' Mum said quickly,

'Yes *what*?'

'Yes, a motorbike accident,' Mum said. 'A tragic motorbike accident.'

Her face had gone absolutely bleak and she looked very pale and very vulnerable — as if one word from me could break her into a million pieces. I didn't like to ask her anything else.

'What's for dinner?' I said instead. 'D'you want me to peel some potatoes?'

By the time Dad came in at dead on six-thirty, she was her normal self. I watched her bustling about, jumping up and down from the table to get whatever he wanted, and thought it was awful that she couldn't be herself, couldn't talk about Melanie in front of him.

I looked at Dad: what did *he* feel? I didn't think I'd ever heard him mentioning Melanie, except in a cutting way when I did something he disapproved of: 'Yes, your sister used to do stupid things like that,' he'd say, or 'Your sister had those same misguided ideas.'

I didn't love him. I didn't even respect him. He was just the man at the head of the table. I could never remember cuddling him or going to him with problems; he wasn't like the dads in the stories or the advertisements, the ones helping with the shopping or getting into a state with the washing machine or teasing their daughters about boys. Especially not that. I couldn't imagine what he'd be like when — if ever — I started going out on dates. He didn't like me having girl friends home; so I didn't think he'd make boys very welcome.

I helped Mum wash up and then I went upstairs to write an essay for Biology and afterwards sat in front of my bedroom mirror fiddling with my hair, thinking about what Nicki had said about doing something with myself.

My room was dire. It was papered with pink and green flowers and had a carpet which had once been in our sitting room downstairs. There was also a huge mahogany wardrobe with a mirror on the front and a kidney-shaped dressing table with a frill of material round it. On the top were some glass containers that were supposed to contain perfume and loose powder and stuff – the whole set was really ancient and used to belong to my gran. There weren't any grans or grandads around any more. Dad was nearly sixty and Mum was fifty-eight, so their parents were long gone. I think I do dimly remember a granny, but she died when I was four.

I stared at myself in the mirror, wondering how Jacko saw me: he'd said he'd marked me out as different from the other girls. Different nice, though, or different frumpy? Ok, my skin's quite good and Nicki had said that my eyes were nice and that if I did something else to my hair it could look OK, but I was just so horribly ordinary.

I pulled my hair up on top of my head, then caught it back at the sides and tried to flick it under to see what it would look like shorter . . . with a different fringe . . . curly. I wanted to look different, I wanted Jacko to really like me. I was fed up with being a rabbit.

Chapter 3

My hair – and the rest of me – was still the same a few days later as I waited, on a Friday and later than usual, for the bus home after school. I'd said something to Mum about having a new hairstyle, maybe going to a salon instead of having Mrs Pearce do it, but she'd said my hairstyle was very suitable for a teenager, and pointed out that a re-style in one of the salons would cost at least ten pounds and she couldn't afford it. At the weekend I was going to buy myself some clips and combs and things, though, and see if I could change my hairstyle that way.

Money was another of the areas where I seemed to be different from the other girls that I knew: I just didn't have any. For ages I'd been wanting a job, a Saturday job, but Dad wouldn't let me get one, said he hadn't insisted that I went to a decent school only to see me on the cash desk in a supermarket on Saturdays.

The bus came along and, the awful mud-brown cloak swirling about me, I got on and sat just inside on the first seat. I began to think about the next morning and whether Jacko would be at the bus stop. I hadn't seen him to talk to all week: once I'd seen him on the bus that was pulling away as I neared the stop, once he'd been chatting to an older man – his dad, I wondered? – and I hadn't liked to do any more than smile at him, and once I hadn't seen him at all.

That didn't mean I hadn't thought a lot about him, though.

I'd shown my bus pass and was just putting it back in my folder when someone came and plonked themselves down right next to me. I looked up in surprise, because the bus wasn't crowded. It was Jacko.

'You're late, aren't you?' he said. 'I've never seen you at this sort of time before.'

I smiled, really pleased to see him. 'They've started a French conversation class at school,' I said, thinking how swotty it sounded, 'and some of us stay behind once in a while and just chat.' The rabbits, mostly. The girls who didn't have anything better to do with themselves.

'Sounds pretty high powered,' he said. 'I dropped French in the fourth year.'

'Do you always finish at this time, then?'

He nodded. 'Officially we finish at four, but a crowd of us doss about for an hour or so just chatting and drinking coffee. We've got a coffee machine and a snack bar where you can buy crisps and stuff.'

I thought about him dossing about, as he put it, and felt the same sort of jab of jealousy that I'd felt before. There would be girls there, of course; girls in his class, girls he chatted to just like he chatted to me.

'Have you got anything like that?'

'Like a coffee machine?' I shook my head. 'We're treated just the same as the rest of the school: like kids. The sixth form is no different.'

'You want to change and come to Greatlands,' he said, 'it's a laugh.'

I made a face. 'I bet my father wouldn't think so.'

'Is it because of him that you're at an all-girls school?'

I nodded. 'I think we moved here because it had the only one in the area.'

'What . . . does he think you'll shrivel away to dust if you see a man?'

I giggled. 'Something like that.'

'If you don't mind me saying, he sounds a real freak.'

'He is!' Funny how I didn't feel disloyal letting someone who was almost a stranger criticize him, but, as I said, I really didn't feel much for my father at all.

'That was my dad I was with at the bus stop the other morning,' Jacko said.

'He looked OK,' He'd been a regular sort of dad, about forty, smart and with a beard. 'He looks like a cornflakes dad,' I added.

Jacko grinned. 'What's a cornflakes dad?'

'One of those you get in the advertisements: a nice, ordinary sort of one.'

'I'll tell him. I take it that yours isn't like that?'

'Not a bit!'

'He's not a vicar or anything, is he?'

I shook my head. 'He works in a bank.'

'He sounds as if he ought to be a vicar: one of those Victorian, thundering ones.'

It was our stop. I got off, conscious of how plain I looked. It had only been lately, about the time I'd first noticed Jacko at the bus stop, that I'd started thinking about my appearance. It felt strange to be so self-conscious.

We got off the bus and I started to say goodbye, knowing Jacko lived in the opposite direction, but as

I did so he said he might as well walk me home. This threw me for a while and I felt all awkward — it was a jump forward I hadn't been expecting — but then I found things to talk to him about and it turned out really well. To begin with anyway. . .

We'd just crossed into my road when I had an awful shock: my father was coming towards us from the direction of the station. He must have caught an earlier train home.

Jacko was still talking — something about a disco at Greatlands — but I could hardly take in what he was saying. I felt grossly uncomfortable about my dad seeing us together but didn't know what to do: I couldn't tell Jacko to hide and I could hardly just leave him and run off. I told myself to calm down . . . it would probably be okay . . . I was only walking along the road with someone I'd met on the bus, after all. I didn't see how even my father could object to that.

It might still have been okay, but at that moment Jacko caught hold of my hand. 'So how about coming to our disco in a couple of weeks?' he said, and I was so completely taken aback that I couldn't do anything else but gawp at him.

My father was getting nearer and nearer. I froze.

'My father. . .' I said in a strangled voice.

Jacko looked towards him. 'Up ahead?'

I nodded.

He squeezed my hand. 'It's okay,' he said carelessly, obviously having no idea of what my father was really like. 'I'll talk to the old geezer . . . chat him up a bit.'

I was about to say I doubted this when my father suddenly realized that the girl coming towards him was his daughter, and she was holding hands with someone he'd never seen before. I saw the actual moment it registered: one second his face was the bland, set mask it usually was, the next his eyes had narrowed, his brow had furrowed and his lips had gone even thinner than they were usually.

We all faced each other outside our front gate.

'Dad, this is...' I began nervously, and Jacko dropped my hand and held his out to shake my father's.

My father just stood there glowering at me and my introductions dried up.

'Go indoors, Joanna,' he said.

I felt my bottom lip begin to tremble. 'I want you to ... to meet...' I began again.

He pointed at the front door. 'I think I told you to go in.'

'Mr ... er ...' Jacko said, and I realized that he didn't know my second name. I couldn't help him; I just looked at him and shook my head helplessly, my eyes filling with tears.

My father ignored Jacko and his outstretched hand. Giving me a dig in the back, he walked behind me to the front door.

I turned and mouthed 'Sorry' to Jacko, who was looking astounded. Well he might: the whole thing had been like a scene from a film.

My father reached round me and put his key in the lock, then pushing me in front of him we went in and he closed the door behind us.

'Upstairs and start your homework, Joanna,' he said as we stood in the hall.

I stared at him angrily, tears blurring my eyes.

'You've just made me look stupid – completely

stupid — in front of . . . of a friend!' I burst out. 'How *could* you?'

'No homework tonight?' he said coolly.

I burst into tears. 'Why did you do that? I was only walking home with someone!'

'That's how these things start. I mean to stop these friendships for your own good.' He looked at me over his glasses. 'You see, I'm trying to prevent what happened to Melanie, happening to you. I've no intention of letting you end up like your sister.'

'What d'you mean, end up like her? What's *she* got to do with anything? This is *me!*' I sobbed.

'Upstairs, Joanna,' he said. 'I can't stand hysterical women.'

I clenched my fists tightly. I felt like pounding him, pounding his stupid striped suit, forcing him to listen to me and understand. I didn't dare touch him, though. I'd had sixteen years of being a rabbit, taking everything he said, obeying without question. Mum came out of the kitchen and I knew she'd been behind the door in there, listening.

'Do go upstairs and calm yourself down, Jo,' she said, and I knew that she was terrified that I'd fight back, cause a scene. 'Just go up for me, love, will you?'

I was a mess of tears; I wouldn't have been able to say anything coherent anyway. I just turned away and did as they wanted; went upstairs and flung myself on my bed.

It was all too awful; I couldn't bear it. To think that he'd asked me out, too. Actually asked me out. What on earth was I going to say when I saw him at the bus stop again?

Suppose he told his friends? Suppose Sara and the

others got to hear? Suppose they laughed about it at school in front of me?

I cried for a while, but the anger I felt burnt up a lot of the tears. In this day and age how could *anyone* be like my father? Maybe I could run away . . . go somewhere and get a live-in job. The way things were going he was never going to let me grow up, become a real person.

When I stopped crying I started to think about what he'd said . . . the words he'd used. Why had he brought Melanie into it? What had he meant by saying that he was trying to prevent what had happened to her, happening to me? Now that I'd started to think about Melanie it felt as though everything concerning her was strange: unreal and woolly. I never seemed to be able to put my finger on the real her and discover what sort of a person she'd been and what had actually happened to her.

Eventually I got up and went into the bathroom to splash my face. Downstairs I could hear – not a row, because Mum never really rowed with Dad – but a discussion going on. Dad's monotonous drone was occasionally broken by a remark from Mum. I crept to the edge of the stairs and it was then that I heard Mum say, very clearly: 'We should have told her, Frank. She'll have to know,' and then my Dad saying dogmatically: 'Never! You tell her and. . .' and then Mum started crying and I couldn't hear anything else.

Chapter 4

'I've got something I want to ask you, Mum,' I said on Monday morning. I'd been brooding about things all weekend and I'd hardly spoken to Dad at all. That wasn't unusual, though; with Dad you often just spoke when you were spoken to.

Mum paused from washing up his cereal bowl. She was wearing furry slippers and a cross-over paisley overall – like the ones you see the women wearing in wartime films.

'What's that, dear?'

I took a breath. 'I want to know what all the mystery about Melanie is.'

She was in the process of lifting the bowl out of the soapy water and putting it onto the draining board. She gave a little start and it slipped out of her hands and crashed into the sink, where it broke.

I looked at her. She was usually so neat and careful in her movements.

'What?'

'About Melanie,' I repeated. 'I'm sorry if talking about it upsets you, but I want to know more about her.'

She got a sheet of newspaper and carefully began to pick the pieces of china out of the sink one by one, then placed them on the paper and rolled it up.

'What did she do that was so bad? Why does Dad say things like I'll end up like her and all that? Just because I was talking to a boy – walking home with one...'

'He's a funny man ... he doesn't mean half the things he says.'

I gave a bitter laugh.

'He thinks a lot of you. He doesn't ... doesn't want anything to happen to you.'

'Well, it won't will it? Just because I'm talking to a boy doesn't mean I'm going to go off on a motor-bike and get myself killed.'

Mum winced.

'Anyway, there was something I heard you saying on Friday. You were talking about me and said there was something you ought to have told me; that I'd have to know. *What?*'

Mum was still a moment, and then turned from the sink, her face perfectly composed and blank.

'I don't know what you're talking about,' she said.

'Mum, I *heard*. There's something you mustn't tell me.'

'You must have misheard.'

'I don't think so.'

'You really shouldn't listen to private conversations, Joanna,' she said, and then she turned her back on me again and I knew I wasn't going to get anything else out of her.

I changed tack. There was another thing which had been puzzling me, something which I'd never really thought about before, but which now I had seemed really strange. 'Where's Melanie buried?' I asked suddenly. 'Why don't we ever go and visit her and put flowers on her grave and all that?'

Mum sat down at the kitchen table wearily; her head resting on her hands. 'She was cremated,' she said in a tired voice. 'Your father and I thought it best. We . . . we knew we'd be moving from the area so we wouldn't have been able to look after the grave.'

'But it just seems so strange when you come to think of it,' I said earnestly, 'I mean, we never. . .'

'Joanna,' Mum interrupted, 'I really don't want to talk about it; you know I find it upsetting.'

'But. . .'

'Also I promised your father that I wouldn't,' she added abruptly. I looked at her set, troubled face and knew it was useless to go on.

I got on with my cereal. I was late for my usual bus, but I'd planned to be. I just couldn't face Jacko; I couldn't even bear to think about seeing him. I'd been over and over the scene outside the house in my mind, and my humiliation and embarrassment hadn't got any less.

'Has Dad always been like he is?' I asked Mum when I'd finished eating, 'Has he always been so strict? Was he like that with her?'

Mum nodded. 'He was just the same with Melanie,' she said. 'He never liked having people in the house and he didn't like Melanie going out.'

'And how did she take that?'

'She didn't, I'm afraid. She was a strong-willed girl; she used to go out and about as much as she wanted and bring her friends home whether he liked it or not. She was a charmer, was Melanie, used to twist him round her little finger – that's why her – her death hit him so hard. It was like a betrayal.'

I was silent for a while. 'So maybe if I'd been firmer from the start, more positive. . .'

Mum shook her head. 'He changed after Melanie.

He was strict before, but he got worse with you. Even when you were quite tiny he expected complete obedience from you. I sometimes think he's being unfair, but there's nothing I can do about it. Nothing you can do about it, either, while you're under his roof.'

I didn't reply; I just went upstairs to clean my teeth and do my hair. There *was* nothing I could do about it, and it would be years before I could leave home. There were no relatives I could go and live with, either: Mum had a sister somewhere in the country but they'd fallen out years ago; they didn't even send each other Christmas cards now.

I left the house and walked to the bus stop – and was relieved to see that the morning rush was over and there was hardly anyone waiting. OK, I knew I could miss tutor group that day and go straight to my first class, but I couldn't miss it for ever. Sooner or later I'd have to see Jacko.

After lunch, coming out of the library, I bumped into Nicki.

'What's up with *you*?' she asked. 'I noticed you in class earlier looking like a wet weekend.'

'Nothing much,' I said. I didn't mind her talking to me like that. She was blunt, but at least she was also straightforward and honest, whereas most of the Beauties were as false as their fingernails.

"Come on,' she said. 'Tell me. Is it that that boy on the bus – Jacko? Has he given you the cold shoulder?'

We walked away from the library building back towards the Sixth block. 'Has he gone off you or something? Didn't I tell you to dress yourself up a bit?'

'I *was* going to,' I said wryly. In the end I hadn't

bothered to do anything with myself: not even go shopping for the things I wanted for my hair. I didn't have the heart, somehow. What would have been the point?

I told her what had happened; it was a relief to be able to tell someone.

'How awful!' she said when I'd finished. 'Haven't you got anyone who can speak out for you – any cousins or grannies or anyone?'

I shook my head.

'What about your mum, then? Or is she as bad?'

'She's as old fashioned,' I said, 'but she's not as strict as my dad.'

'Wouldn't she say something to him? Try and help?'

I pushed open the door of the sixth-form block. 'Nope! She's scared of him, too. She's like a mouse.'

'I'll come round if you like!' Nicki said. 'Maybe I could say something . . . point out how unreasonable he's being.'

'Don't you dare!' I managed to smile at her. 'Thanks all the same but you'd only make things worse.'

'I think you ought to rebel!' she said.

I was shaking my head almost before she'd finished the sentence. 'I can't! I'd be too scared to.'

'There must be someone who could say something to him. Haven't you got any brothers or sisters?'

'Not now. There was someone . . . I had an older sister, you see, but she died.'

'How?' Nicki asked bluntly.

'Some sort of accident on her boyfriend's motorbike.'

'*She* was allowed boyfriends, then?'

'She wasn't – but she had one all the same. The thing is. . .'

'What?' Nicki prompted.

'There's some sort of mystery about her. There are no photos around or anything, and because we haven't got any relatives, no one ever speaks about her – except for Mum sometimes, and she always cries when she does.'

'Hmm.' Nicki said, looking thoughtful.

'What are you thinking?' I asked her.

'Well,' she said, 'it's probably far-fetched and ridiculous, and I'm always being told I'm over-imaginative, but if your father's got an awful temper and is dead strict and everything, suppose he and your sister had a terrible row and he killed her accidentally and that's why it's all hush-hush?'

My jaw dropped. I suppose if I'd liked my father I might have been offended, but as it was, I was just taken aback. Such a thought had never occurred to me.

'You said once that you all moved house after she died . . . that could be why. And if there's a big ban on talking about her. . .'

I shook my head slowly. 'Surely not. Not really. Normal people. . .'

'Normal people *do*. Things like that happen in the most ordinary families, that's just it.'

I opened my mouth and shut it again. It was too much to take in. I knew he was strict, I knew he sometimes had a temper and was stern and unbending, but surely. . .

'Maybe you'd better not rebel after all,' Nicki said, raising her eyebrows. 'Maybe you'd better just sit tight and put up with it all until you're older and you can get away.'

The bell went, signalling the end of lunchtime. Sara's little group began to break up.

I sighed. My father and Melanie . . . it couldn't be true. I didn't even want to think about it. There was something I *had* to think about though. 'What am I going to do when I see Jacko again?' I asked her. 'I can't avoid him by being late for school every day.'

She shook her head. 'I don't know. I hate to say this, but you may not have to say anything: if he's like any of the boys I know he'll probably run a mile.'

I nodded. Of course. I wouldn't have to say anything because there was no need for *him* to put up with my father – and me – when he didn't have to. He'd obviously just cut me dead next time I happened to see him at the bus stop.

Chapter 5

As I waited at the bus stop on Friday morning there was a tap on my shoulder which made me jump.

'I think you've been avoiding me,' a voice said. 'I've been on time every morning this week but you haven't been here.'

I wheeled round. It was Jacko in his bright blue skiing jacket, his hair looking newly washed and fluffy.

'I wondered if you'd started going into school later, so I thought I'd hang about a bit this morning and find out.'

'Oh,' I said. I felt myself going as red as a beetroot.

'Of course,' he shrugged, 'if you've been trying to give me the slip, if you don't want to chat, you've only got to say so and I'll beat it.'

'Oh no!' I said, horrified that he might think I was trying to avoid him because I didn't like him. 'It's not that.' I felt another wave of colour sweep over me. 'It's just . . . well, because of what happened last week – my father. I didn't want to face you.'

'So you've been going in late deliberately, just because of him? Because you felt embarrassed?'

I nodded.

'And there's me been hanging about, missing buses and getting into trouble. . .'

'Sorry!' I said and beamed at him, suddenly feeling

brilliantly happy. So Nicki didn't know everything about boys – *he hadn't* wanted to make a run for it.

'The way I look at it is this,' he said, 'you can't help having an ogre for a father any more than I can help having a cornflakes dad, can you?'

I smiled. Jacko could even make having a father like mine seem funny. Well, he *was* an ogre. There was no other word for him.

'None of us can help our relations. I mean, I've got some pretty dodgy aunts – aunts I wouldn't want to be seen out in daylight with. They're not my fault, though, are they?'

I giggled; a bus came along and we got on it and sat together.

'So – tell me about him,' Jacko said as the bus moved off through the traffic. 'Give me the lowdown.'

I explained as best I could about my mother and father, about them being years older than anyone else's parents and about how I'd grown up feeling different from girls my own age. Jacko was great to talk to; I never thought I was boring him or that he might be laughing at me behind my back like I did with some of the girls at school, he just seemed really interested and concerned, stopping me every now and then to ask a question or get me to explain something more fully.

I told him about Melanie.

'There's a girl at school – Nicki – well, she's got this theory about my sister.' I lowered my voice. 'I mean, I don't think it could possibly be true but she says that because my father's so ridiculously strict and because there's a lot of secrecy about Melanie they've obviously got something to hide ... she reckons my father had a violent fight with Melanie and hit her or something, and she died.'

Jacko whistled. '*Has* he got a temper?'

'Not *that* bad, I don't think. I mean, he's pretty grim and stern, but he's like that all the time; he doesn't often just flare up.'

'Could you find out any more? What about relations?'

I shook my head. 'There aren't any.'

'Neighbours from where you used to live?'

'I don't even know where that was.'

'We could find out. There's bound to be someone still around who'll remember your family ... especially if they had a daughter who died.'

I stared at him. 'I don't know if I'd dare.'

'I'd help. I'd be with you.' My hand was on my lap, nervously clutching my school bag and he put his own hand over it and squeezed it gently.

I was overcome for a moment and then I looked up and gave a little yelp: we were almost at the school stop. 'I've got to get off!'

He released my hand and dived into his inside pocket for some paper and a pencil. 'Here's my number at home. If you ever need me, ring me up.'

He scribbled something down and I took the piece of paper and stood up. 'And I'll see you tomorrow morning!' he said. 'No more messing about and making us both late.'

'I'm stopping for French tonight,' I said tentatively.

'Great! I'll see you about a quarter to five, then. I'll be outside your school.'

The driver was glowering at me, impatient to be off, and I ran down the bus and jumped off just as the doors were closing. I was seeing him again, that actual afternoon! It was practically a date.

I would have been late for tutor group again so I cut that and went straight to Biology. Sara must have missed tutor group, too, because she was already in the lab.

'I really don't know what things are coming to,' she said loudly as I walked in, 'to think that little Miss Rabbit keeps missing tutor group these mornings!'

I felt that nothing could deflate me right then; I just smiled at her and went to my seat.

'We must really have something important on to stop us missing it, mustn't we?'

I really hated the smarmy way she spoke to me but I just tried to ignore her.

'And I do believe I know what it is.' She examined her nails lazily. 'It's Jacko, isn't it? You've been meeting him in the mornings. That's why you've been late this week.'

'No, it isn't,' I said.

She shook her head and the golden halo of hair stood out. 'Now, we mustn't tell lies!' she said coyly. 'You were seen on the bus again.'

'Well, this morning I did, but it wasn't...' I stopped. I didn't see why I had to tell her anything.

'Holding hands, I daresay!' she said in a silly, coy voice.

I went pink. She didn't know anything; I was willing to bet that she didn't even know we'd been on the bus together that morning, she just wanted to make me feel uncomfortable.

'Oh yes, holding hands,' she said, seeing me go pink. 'And a little kiss on the cheek goodbye as well!'

Now I knew she hadn't seen me. I pretended to be

busy getting out my biology notes and going through them but she came over to the bench where I was and bent over me.

'You want to watch it, you know, Joanna McIver,' she said. 'Don't kid yourself that Jacko is the slightest bit interested in a frump like you.'

I managed to keep my head down and started copying something we'd learnt last week.

'My friend Danielle at home fancies Jacko – and he fancies her. Don't you start interfering in *that*.'

I swallowed hard. I felt tears begin to come into my eyes but I fought not to let them show.

'So just you keep off,' she said nastily, 'because he belongs to someone else.'

Mrs Layfield, our biology teacher, came into the room then, followed by the rest of the class. Sara, stung because she hadn't caused any reaction in me, nudged my arm violently so I streaked my page with blue ink, and then walked away.

I felt miserable for the rest of the day. I didn't know whether what Sara had said about her friend Danielle and Jacko was true, but in any case it just felt as if what had happened that morning had been spoilt. For that short time I'd felt brilliantly happy; being with Jacko had given me a cosy sort of feeling, as if I had someone of my own who was actually bothered about me; a friend. I didn't think my father cared for me a bit – and though my mum obviously did, it was Dad who came first every time with her; she wasn't prepared to stick up for me against him. Before Sara had said her little piece, though, I'd felt that Jacko might.

In spite of what Sara had said, and even if Jacko *did* have someone else, I still wanted to look good when I met him, so as I had a few minutes spare after French Conversation, I went into the cloakrooms to try and do something with myself.

I stared at my reflection in the smeary mirrors above the sinks. Looking at myself hard, it was awfully difficult to believe that someone like Jacko was interested in me. I was always pale, but that day I seemed extra pale, my eyes standing out big and dark and my hair hanging long, straight and straggly. I had a brush in my pocket and I pulled it through again and again until the tangles were smoothed out and it started to shine. I wasn't exactly going to knock him dead, but as I didn't have a change of clothes or any make-up on me, this was all I could do.

Going out of the school I felt dead nervous. OK, so it wasn't a date, but it was the first time any boy had arranged to meet me.

He was waiting just by the gate. I wished to myself that Sara could be there to see him waiting, and then I thought that it was just as well she wasn't – she'd only have another go at me.

' 'Ello,' he said, taking my hand and kissing it. 'You 'ave made ze French conversation, yes?'

I laughed and nodded.

'And now we go togezzer to ze autobus stop.'

We walked along chatting. Jacko was speaking pretend French all the time, which made it easy to say what I wanted to.

'You've got a friend with a French name, haven't you?' I said. 'Danielle.'

'Yeah!' He didn't look taken aback or anything. 'She's doing one of the catering courses at Greatlands. You know her, do you?'

I shook my head. 'She's a friend of a . . . er friend. Sara at school knows her.'

'Sara Batting? Yeah, that's her best mate. A couple of right ones, they are.'

I puzzled over this as we stood at the bus stop. Right ones . . . it didn't sound as if he liked them.

'They come to everything that's going on – all the discos and social events and trips. All over the place, they are.'

'Are they a laugh?' I tried to sound nonchalant, 'Do you like them?'

'Not a lot. Sorry if she's a mate of yours but they're a couple of cats – always slagging people off and trying to stir up trouble.'

I looked at him: did I believe what he was saying, or did I believe Sara? Well, there was no choice.

'So, what are we going to do about the ogre?' he said when we were on the bus. 'What shall I do – come and have a face-to-face with him?'

'You wouldn't get as far as the front door!'

'And by the way – last Friday, just when he was in the middle of springing and breathing fire I was asking you to come to our disco. How are you fixed for next Saturday?'

I shook my head slowly. 'I'd like to . . . I'd really like to, but I just can't. He'd never let me go to a disco.'

'What if I did it the proper way . . . the formal way. What if I came round, knocked at your door and asked to escort you. He couldn't object to that, surely?'

'You wouldn't. . .' I faltered, 'you wouldn't want to do all that.'

'I wouldn't mind! I'd look upon it as a challenge.'

'I still don't think he'd let me go.'

'D'you want me to try?'

I smiled at him. I'd *love* him to try; I'd love to dress up and go to a disco, dance with him, maybe end the evening kissing him goodnight...

'I will, then,' he said, though I hadn't actually replied in words.

When we got off the bus I asked him not to walk me home again, but we stood for a while at the bus stop talking about his coming round to see my father, 'For him, I'll even wear my interview suit!' he said, 'and as it's a really special occasion – no trainers! I always find a proper pair of shoes goes down well with ogres.' He took my hand. 'And in the meantime, see if you can find out anything else about this sister of yours and solve that mystery,' he said, 'Why not ask your mum about where you used to live?'

I nodded. 'I might be able to find out more than that,' I said. 'Mum said that in the attic there's a whole boxful of Melanie's stuff that she couldn't bring herself to throw away. If I could get up there ... maybe there are photographs, diaries... I could find out what sort of relationship she had with my father – whether they fought a lot, stuff like that.'

'That's it,' he said. 'Anything which will help us figure out what happened to her. I reckon if we can find out more about *her*, we'll find out more about your dad and learn how we ought to handle him.'

He squeezed my hand. 'You're quite a challenge, Jo,' he said, 'but I've always fancied being a knight in shining armour.'

'This is a pretty funny princess's get up, though, 'I said, looking down at the gruesome uniform and cringing.

'It's what's inside it that counts,' he said, 'and that looks pretty good to me.'

As I walked home on my own, those last few words were all I could think about. I could hardly believe it, it was completely incredible, but it seemed as if he really liked me...

Chapter 6

'For what we are about to receive, may the Lord make us truly thankful,' my father intoned from the head of the dining table. It was Thursday night but it could have been any night: we always sat down at the same time, in the same places, and he always said Grace before we were allowed to start.

I cast a nervous eye at the clock on the mantelpiece. It was six-thirty now; we'd probably get up from the table at ten to seven. At seven o'clock, when I'd be helping Mum with the washing up and Dad would just have gone into the sitting room to listen to the news, Jacko was coming round. With luck, Dad would be in a fairly decent mood, decent enough to give Jacko a fair hearing perhaps, and to actually listen to what he had to say instead of jumping to conclusions and making vast generalizations about me and my sister.

I looked at Dad from out of the corner of my eye: he had his eyes closed and his lips were moving slightly as if he was praying. All that praying business didn't fool me, though. Oh, he went to church on Sundays and watched the religious programmes in the evening, but as for being Christian, really caring about his fellow man – well, I'd never seen him lift a hand to help anyone or even say anything kind or sympathetic. Whenever people were in trouble he said they must have 'brought it on themselves'; that was one of his favourite expressions.

'Pass the condiments please, Joanna,' he said when he opened his eyes, and I dutifully passed them along. We weren't allowed to stretch for things, we always had to ask, and we weren't allowed to start eating until we were sure that everyone (i.e. my father) had whatever he wanted. Condiments! Whoever called them that now, anyway?

I'd seen Jacko quite a bit that week. Not to go out with properly of course, but on the bus and after school a couple of times. The more I saw him, the more I liked him and the more things I found we had in common. I wouldn't have thought it possible that I'd have had much in common with someone like Jacko, someone who'd led an ordinary sort of life, going out and about whenever he wanted and having friends around and all that, but deep down there was something about us that was the same. I didn't know what it was: it was an inner thing, not an outer thing.

We'd been planning tonight's confrontation for a couple of days. I was all for leaving well alone; I think I was scared that if Dad did hit the roof again, Jacko would be frightened off for good and not want to bother about me, but he'd insisted.

'Some time I want to take you out properly,' he'd said at the bus stop the day before, 'not just see you on buses.'

'At least seeing each other on buses is *something*,' I'd said, 'Suppose when he finds out that we're meeting, he stops it altogether?'

'Short of chaining you up all day, how's he going to do that?'

I'd shrugged. 'I wouldn't put anything past him.'

Jacko had shaken his head. 'He's not going to do anything to stop us seeing each other,' he'd said, 'because I just wouldn't take any notice.' He'd looked me straight in the eye, 'Would you?' he asked sternly.

I'd shaken my head because I'd known he wanted me to, but privately I wondered to myself how I was suddenly going to get the courage to stand up to my father after sixteen years of obeying whatever he said.

'It'll be OK,' he'd said softly. 'Really it will. I'll be polite, I'll say the right things, I'll be Mr Straight.'

I'd laughed, unable to see Jacko as Mr Straight.

'I won't mention the disco . . . I'll say we're going to a . . . what's a real squarish sort of thing? A performance of Handel's Messiah!'

'In October?'

'What *shall* I say, then?'

'Just say . . . say you'd like to take me out. You needn't say where. He probably doesn't know what a disco, is, anyway.'

'He must do!'

'He's the original ostrich with his head in the sand.'

Jacko had shaken his head. 'What a family! Jo McIver, you're a real odd-ball, you know that?'

For a moment I felt miserable: I was the odd one out, the onlooker, the outsider. I always had been and probably always would be. But Jacko had seen my face fall. 'It's OK. I positively like odd-balls,' he'd said, taking my hand. 'You're different from every girl I've ever met but that's probably why I fancy you so much.'

I'd felt better again immediately. He fancied me! I'd clutched his hand and it felt like a lifeline out of my old gloomy life and into his happy one.

Dad coughed slightly and I came back to reality.

'Everything all right, dear?' Mum asked him, and he nodded majestically.

'Very nice,' he said, 'although perhaps the gravy is a trifle thin.'

I swallowed down my irritation. Nothing was ever completely right: either the potatoes had a strange flavour or the meat was a little tough or the greens were just slightly over-salted. I'd come to the conclusion that it was impossible to please him.

'Everything all right at school, Joanna?' he asked me.

I nodded. 'Fine.'

'Because this year is probably your most important one. Whatever happens you mustn't slacken.'

I nodded agreement, most of my mind taken up with the clock on the mantelpiece ... only fifteen minutes and Jacko would be here. Anyway, my father had said the same thing every year since I'd started school – that *this* year was going to be my most important one.

I searched my mind for something to talk to him about, something about school which might put him in a good mood.

'Mrs Salter says my French is coming on a treat,' I blurted.

' "Coming on a treat"?' he said. 'What sort of an expression is that?'

'You know your father doesn't like slang, dear.'

'I mean, she thinks it's really improved since the beginning of this term. She reckons I should get a good "A" level grade.'

'I'm glad to hear it,' my father said.

'Languages are always useful,' Mum put in. 'Whatever you do, a second language will be helpful.'

'Oh – and there's a trip to France just before Christmas,' I said, 'there'll be a letter home about it. We've got to go this year, apparently, because next year we'll be studying for our mocks and then the real exams and there wouldn't be time.'

'That'll be nice,' Mum said. 'How long will it be for?'

'Only six days,' I said, 'but Mrs Salter said it'll really help our pronunciation. We're not allowed to speak anything but French the whole time.'

'Will it be properly supervised?' my father asked.

I nodded vehemently. 'They're going to stay in a place which was once a French convent. There are only nine of us doing French "A" level anyway, and two teachers are going so we'll be well looked after.'

Mum shot a look at my father. 'Well, that sounds all right, doesn't it? Do you think Joanna will be able to go?'

'Probably . . . probably,' he said, 'though I'll have to find out more about it first.'

I forced some more food down, though I didn't feel hungry. I hadn't thought much about the trip to France; I'd been too busy thinking about Jacko lately, but it would be wonderful if I could go. Six days on my own; six days without my father breathing down my neck; six days to just do my own thing.

There was a ring on the doorbell and I jumped. It couldn't be Jacko already, surely! I glanced at the clock: he was much too early, my father hadn't even finished eating.

'I'll go,' I said, jumping up.

'You haven't finished,' my father said, nodding at my place for me to sit down again. 'I do hate interruptions when we're at the table.'

I sat down, put the last piece of meat in my mouth. 'I've finished now,' I said.

'Shall I go, dear?' Mum said. 'It's probably only someone selling something.'

I started to feel shaky. I should never have let him come; it was doomed to disaster, I knew it was. 'I'll go,' I said. I'd have to tell him to go away; I couldn't go through with it.

My father calmly wiped round his plate with a cube of potato. 'Whoever it is, we're not interested,' he said.

I ran into the hall and opened the front door. Jacko stood there smiling nervously. He looked different: scrubbed, squeaky clean, his hair brushed flat, his white shirt and jacket looking as out of place on him as would a pair of jeans on my father.

'What are you doing? You weren't supposed to answer the door,' he hissed.

I could hardly speak for nerves. 'It's OK,' I gabbled, 'I've changed my mind,'

'What!?'

'We'll do it another time. Not now.'

'Jo!' He looked at me pleadingly. 'Come on, I haven't got myself all dressed up like a dog's dinner for nothing!'

I looked at him standing there, a perfect Mr Straight, and didn't know whether to laugh or cry. *He was doing all this for me!*

'Who is it, Joanna?' came my father's voice from the dining room.

'No one!' I called back.

'Jo,' Jacko said, 'it'll be OK, I'm sure he'll be reasonable. I've only come to see if he'll let you go on a date with me, I'm not going to abduct you or anything. He's got to listen to me.'

'No. He won't. Just go!' I said urgently.

I heard my father's chair scrape back on the wooden floor of the dining room and I looked at Jacko bleakly. It was too late.

My father came into the hall and walked along to the front door, and with each step he took I felt I wanted to die.

'Yes?' he said to Jacko.

'Good evening, Mr McIver,' Jacko said formally, 'I'm a friend of Joanna's.'

'I wasn't aware that she had any male friends.'

'Yes, well, my name's Michael Jackson and I go to Greatlands. I wondered if you would mind if I took Joanna out some evening.'

My father was silent.

Jacko coughed nervously and my heart went out to him. If I didn't love him before, I started to love him right then.

'Go out to a ... er ... concert or something. I'd have her home at whatever time you ... er ... stipulated.'

I held my breath.

'I am sorry,' my father said, 'but Joanna does not go out with boys.'

I wasn't surprised or even disappointed – after all, it was what I'd been expecting. Just go now, I silently begged Jacko. Give up and go.

'Well, perhaps you might allow me to call round occasionally, then.'

'I most certainly would *not*.'

I could see that Jacko was now at a loss. I began

to shrink back against the wall, frightened of what might happen next.

'But surely, Mr McIver, you'll let us see each other sometimes. You must see that. . .'

'I beg your pardon,' my father said, 'but I must see nothing. I will not be spoken to like this; I will certainly not be told what my daughter can or cannot do by a lout like you.'

Jacko opened his mouth and shut it again.

'And if you'll kindly get your foot out of my door I'll be able to shut it.'

'Dad. . .' I began, but he didn't seem to hear me.

'Mr McIver, I really feel. . .' Jacko said, but my father shut the door in his face, pushing his foot out at the same time, and then strode back into the dining room.

My heart thumping as if I'd run a marathon, I stood and watched Jacko through the glass, praying that he wouldn't thump at the door or do anything silly. He held his ground a moment or two, as if he was stunned, and then he turned and walked away.

'In here, Joanna, please,' my father called.

I went into the dining room. I felt weak with misery; humiliated and beaten. It had all failed miserably, as I'd known it would. My father was never going to let me go out with anyone; he was going to keep me there forever: the dutiful daughter at her aged parents' beck and call. They'd lost one daughter, so they were going to make doubly sure they hung on to me.

'Please don't encourage any more callers,' he said calmly, passing the salt and pepper back through the hatch to Mum.

'You can't keep me in for ever,' I said, suddenly

finding the strength to be defiant. 'I've got to be allowed to have friends of my own.'

'You're too young for that sort of thing. I won't have you going out with boys.'

'I'm sixteen. I'm not a baby!'

'You're too young to know what you're doing.'

In the kitchen I heard Mum clattering pots and pans, trying to drown the sound of our voices; trying to be another ostrich.

'I especially won't have you making friends of that type. I can see what sort of boy he is.'

'He's no *sort* of boy!' I said angrily. 'He's nice . . . decent.'

'I know his type. He's the sort of boy your sister used to go out with. The sort who got her into trouble.'

I stopped being angry for a moment, suddenly interested in the words he'd used. 'What d'you mean?'

'Never you mind what I mean. It's enough to say that there'll be no going out with boys all the time you're under my roof.'

'But Dad, how can you say that? I. . .'

He narrowed his eyes. 'And that's final. There will be no more said on the subject.'

Chapter 7

'We'll be a couple of hours, Joanna,' my mother called up the stairs on Saturday morning. 'Will you be all right?'

'Of course I will,' I called down.

'No using the telephone while we're out,' my father said just before the front door closed behind them.

I ignored him; who did he think I was going to ring anyway, seeing as he'd put paid to me having any friends?

Actually, though he didn't know it, I'd made a phone call to Jacko that morning while he'd been out doing something in the garden. I'd seen Jacko just briefly the morning before: I'd been squeezed onto the platform of the bus when he'd come running down the road. The bus had taken off without him but he'd noticed me, waved madly and then given me a down-thumbs sign and a funny grimace.

It was enough; it said to me that it was hard luck about my father but it didn't make any difference – he still liked me.

I still really wanted to talk to him, though, so when Mum had gone shopping I'd stretched the phone cord as far as it would go from the hall into our sitting room so I could keep an eye on my father in the garden, and dialled the number Jacko had written down for me on the scrap of paper.

'It's Jo,' I'd said a bit nervously when he answered.

'Hi!' He'd seemed genuinely pleased to hear from me. 'I wondered if you'd be able to ring. Has the ogre gone out?'

'He's in the garden. I won't be able to be long.'

'So how was he after I left.'

'Ogreish;' I'd put on my father's pompous voice: ' "Please don't encourage any more callers." '

'He's priceless; he really is!' There was a pause. 'Sorry, Jo. Did I make it worse for you?'

'It doesn't matter. I don't care about what he's like to me really. He's always been like that; it's not something new.'

'We'll have to think of another way of meeting.'

'I could give up French conversation classes,' I'd suggested tentatively, 'they're not very often, though.' Of course it wouldn't be enough for Jacko; he'd want a real girlfriend, someone he could take out places.

'I don't want you to get into trouble because of me.'

I sighed. 'I'm just scared he'll realize that we're meeting at the bus stop and start insisting on accompanying me to school or something.'

Jacko groaned. 'Might he take you in the car?'

'We haven't got a car!'

'Don't tell me: he doesn't believe in motorized vehicles . . . he's got a pony and trap!'

I laughed. 'They've got bus passes and rail passes. He says it's not worth having a car these days.'

'Yeah. That's the sort of thing he would say.'

I'd hesitated. 'Shall I see you on Monday morning, then?'

'Sure thing. Wait for me, will you – and Jo?'

'Mmm?'

'Try and find out a bit more about Melanie. Get up into your loft if you get the chance.'

That reminded me. 'Guess what he said after you went on Thursday. . .' I said, and I'd told him my father's comment about Melanie and the sort of boy who had 'got her into trouble'.

'Sounds interesting. Maybe you'll be able to find out some more.'

'I'll try.' I looked into the garden. 'I'd better go. Have a good time tonight,' I'd added wistfully, thinking about the disco. Sara and her friend Danielle would be bound to be there. Maybe he'd dance with Danielle, buy her a drink, sit at her table. . .

'Wish you were coming to the disco,' he'd said, as if he'd known what I was thinking.

'*I* wish I was coming.'

'Soon. . .'

My father had turned to come in then so I'd said goodbye hurriedly and gone back into the kitchen. Shortly after that, Mum had come back from shopping, we'd had lunch and then they'd announced that they were taking a walk up to the library – something they did occasionally on a Saturday afternoon.

As soon as the door closed behind them I raced up the stairs, tugged the loft ladder down and climbed up. It was dark, but my father had placed a torch just inside the slide-back hatchway, so I put it on and heaved myself up.

The loft was stuffy and close. I'd never been allowed to do dangerous things like climbing loft ladders, so I could only remember looking up there once before, when I'd been little, and as it hadn't looked particularly inviting I hadn't bothered since.

Various strange shapes stood around: old pieces of

furniture, water tanks, vast empty cardboard boxes. There was also an old standard lamp, a tin chest, a vast old radiogram and some packing cases, and I carefully made my way along the roof joists to the nearest of these. I delved into it but it held nothing but old curtains and blankets wrapped in polythene together with, judging from the smell, a vast quantity of mothballs.

The second was the one I was looking for. On the top was a thick cotton sheet, tucked down tightly, but when I pulled up a corner and shone my torch inside, this revealed all sorts of interesting things: a small pile of books tied up with string, some rolled-up pictures or posters, a photograph album, what looked like a dress, some LPs, pop magazines, a large flat box with paper falling out of it and lots of other intriguing shapes and bundles lower down.

My heart started beating very quickly. Here was Melanie ... she had actually existed. All the things which had been important to her in the last year of her life were in this box. My sister Melanie ... I could get to know her at last.

I didn't know where to start. I longed to drag the box downstairs and examine its contents at leisure, but I didn't dare. Mum and Dad might be out as long as an hour, but I couldn't bank on it. I propped the torch up on the edge of the box so that its light shone up on the beams of the roof and pushed my hand into the packing case as if it was a lucky dip.

I unrolled the dress first. It wasn't just a dress, actually; there were several items of clothing: a shaggy looking jacket made out of something like sheepskin with long fringes on it, a pair of flared silky trousers, a pair of shoes with ugly platform heels, a tiny little mini-skirt and the dress itself which the other things had been rolled up in. I held it up and shook it out: it was of thin cotton, flowery, with what looked like a split right up the front. Something fell out onto the floor: a pair of matching shorts. We'd done some work on fashion at school a couple of years ago, so I knew what the outfit was – a hot pants suit. I picked up the shorts – they were tiny, like a pair of knickers ... what on earth had my father thought about Melanie going out in *them*? Had they been her favourite outfit back in 1972, I wondered?

I picked up the photograph album next; this was what I was really looking forward to examining. It was a red plastic one, with transparent leaves inside displaying eight photographs on a page. As far I knew my father didn't have a camera so maybe it had been Melanie's own. I picked up the torch and shone it on the first page, finding Melanie straight away because she was wearing the hot pants outfit. My hand holding the torch shook: it was like looking at a miniature of myself! Oh, the clothes were bizarre, the hair was different, and the way she stood there with her hands on her hips pouting at the camera wasn't like me at all, but her face was my face: high cheekbones, slightly slanting eyes, thick eyebrows, my thick hair – I was a replica of her.

Maybe that was one of the reasons why my father was so possessive, so *ridiculously* possessive with me: because Melanie had once been the apple of his eye. If I was the absolute image of her, then naturally I'd remind him all the time of what he'd lost, so he'd be doubly, triply determined to hang on to me. I slowly turned the pages of the book, thinking deeply. OK,

I could see his point, but it didn't excuse him from ruining my life.

There weren't so many pictures of Melanie – I guessed she'd probably been taking most of them – but there were a whole variety of her friends: masses of friends, colourful boys with really long hair, and girls in tiny little mini skirts or flared trousers with patterned tops and, in a couple of cases, flowers in their hair.

There seemed to be more of one boy in particular ... I wondered if he had been a special one – and then in the middle of the album I saw a close up of him and Melanie together with their arms round each other, looking at each other in such a way that I knew they must have been in love. This was Melanie's boyfriend, then ... perhaps the one who'd caused her death in the motorbike crash. It was funny that there were no motorbikes in any of the photographs, though. Her crowd didn't look as if they were bikers – there were no crash helmets or leather jackets around.

There were some photographs taken at the zoo: Melanie and four or five friends having a picnic with an elephant in the background, the boy and two other girls riding on a camel, then one of Melanie outside a large cage, smiling and pointing to a sign which read: 'Chi Chi our famous panda is very old and may not appear today.'

I turned the pages quickly, wondering if I could take the album downstairs and keep it with me. Maybe there were things written on the back of the photographs: I might be able to find out the boy's name. There were some taken outside a house, too – maybe that had been the house where we'd lived ...

there was a chance that I'd see the name of a road, or perhaps someone might recognize the area. I put the album to one side, picked up the books. They were a mixture: school books and classics like *Wuthering Heights* together with blockbusters with lurid covers. There was also a copy of *Watership Down* with Melanie's name inside and a scrawled note in pencil: 'I loved this book!'

She was getting more real by the minute. I picked up the posters and unrolled them. There were four: three of them I knew – The Jackson Five with Michael Jackson looking cute and chubby, David Bowie in a star-spangled suit and orange hair, and Don McLean bent over a guitar. The other group had very long hair and looked hippyish and American and I'd never seen them before. With the LPs were two singles, Don McLean's 'The Day the Music Died' and 'Starry, Starry Night' – both of which I knew and loved.

There were some magazines and colour supplements and I just looked at the covers hurriedly: Prince Charles getting something from the Queen, a mask of Tutankhamen, the Olympics, a big thing about the Common Market.

I found a large cardboard envelope which I opened up. Inside was a glossy black and white photograph of Melanie in the hot pants outfit with another girl and – I recognized him at once – David Bowie. He held an autograph book in his hand and Melanie was looking up at him devotedly while he signed. I smiled: Melanie looked so nice, like me but with something extra, something indescribable. Like I could be if I was allowed to be me, perhaps.

I looked down at the clothes at my feet. There was

a lot left in the packing case, some intriguing papers and what might be a diary – and I still hadn't found out how or exactly when she'd died – but I had an irresistible urge to try on the hot pants suit and see what I looked like. I laid the torch down on the floor, slipped out of my shirt and blouse and pulled on the shorts. They were skimpy and tight but they fitted all right – and so did the dress. It had been calf-length in the photographs and it was calf-length on me, so Melanie must have been my height.

I looked down at myself but I couldn't really see what I looked like, so on a mad impulse I climbed down the loft ladder and ran into my bedroom, taking the photograph album with me. In one of the photographs Melanie had her hair – which was longer and curlier than mine – caught up at the back, so I fixed mine back in an elastic band and, holding the album at arm's length, stared first at myself in the mirror and then at the photograph.

I gasped: the resemblance was quite amazing – we were like twins.

There was the sound of a key in the lock; I froze.

'We're home, dear!' came Mum's voice.

Panic-stricken, I moved noiselessly towards the landing: I had to get back in the loft, get this off and come down again before they realized I wasn't in my room. With a bit of luck, if they stayed downstairs, I should do it. I hesitated, then I bent down and slid the photograph album under my bed.

I heard them both go into the kitchen. I stepped out onto the landing, put my hand on the loft ladder – and just then my father came out, paused at the bottom of the stairs and looked up and saw me.

I've heard people say things like 'I nearly died' or

'I wished the ground would open up and swallow me', but up until then those words had had no real meaning for me; they'd just been a meaningless cliché, something you said. At that moment, though, the moment he saw me, I really did feel so horrified, devastated and frightened that I wanted to die. I saw my father's face grow white.

'Melanie. . . ?' he asked in a harsh, grating voice, and my mother rushed out of the kitchen to stand by his side and stare up the stairs, horrified.

'It's me. Joanna,' I said.

Mum gave a little scream.

'I found . . . I went up into the loft. . .' I stuttered, and then my mother fainted.

Chapter 8

'What's that strange thing you've got on?' Nicki asked, studying the photograph I was holding out to her. 'And who are all *this* lot. They don't come from round here, do they?'

I smiled. 'Look again.'

'And your hair's different...' She looked from me to the photograph again; 'It's not you!'

I shook my head. 'It's my sister. It's Melanie.'

'Wow!' She took the photograph over to the window so she could examine it in a better light.

'Where did you find it?'

I told her about the box in the loft and then about me trying on the clothes and Mum and Dad coming home in the middle of it.

'It all went a bit mad, then,' I finished. 'Dad came over all peculiar and Mum fainted ... so while he was fussing over her I took the opportunity to nip up the loft ladder, change back into my normal clothes and come back down again.'

Nicki stared at me wide-eyed. 'What happened then?'

'Not a lot. Mum just kept crying and saying "How could you do that to us, Jo?" and Dad kept striding about pounding his fist into his hand and muttering but not really saying anything. It took nearly all weekend for things to get back to normal. Or what passes for normal in our house.'

'I bet!' Nicki breathed. She shook her head wonderingly. 'They must have thought you were a ghost. . .'

'I suppose so. I just wanted to see if I was as much like her as I thought I was.'

'And you obviously were. No wonder your mum fainted!'

I nodded. 'I felt a bit rotten about that.'

'So did you find out anything else?' she asked eagerly. 'About how she died or anything?'

I shook my head. 'Nothing. There were just a lot of things to do with her . . . clothes and records and stuff. As if when she died, Mum had gathered up all her favourite bits and pieces and kept them.'

'If she and your dad did have a fight,' Nicki said, low and excited, 'I mean, I'm not saying he killed her deliberately, but just say he hit her and she fell and knocked her head or something – that happens all the time in the films – he must have thought she'd come back to haunt him!'

I nodded. 'Maybe.'

'Or maybe. . .' Nicki said in a hushed whisper, 'What?'

'Maybe she's not dead at all!'

I stared at her.

'I mean, that must have occurred to you.'

For a moment or two I couldn't speak, only go on staring at her. It *hadn't* occurred to me. I'd grown up as an only child, thinking my sister was dead, and it hadn't crossed my mind to question it. I'd always just believed what I'd been told about her. 'But . . . but why should they pretend she was dead if she wasn't?'

Nicki shrugged. 'All sorts of reasons. They fell out

with her and there was a terrible row . . . she walked out and said she was never coming back. Families do split up, don't they?'

'But I can't believe that my mum would let her go just like that. She was only sixteen!'

'Maybe Melanie let *them* go. Maybe one day she just walked out and your dad was so bitter about it and your mum so hurt that they decided to pretend she was dead.'

I nodded slowly. It was possible, I could see that. It was also weird – but I was beginning to realize that my family *were* weird.

'You said there were some papers and stuff lower down in the box,' Nicki said excitedly. 'You'll have to go up again and dig them out!'

'My father will probably chuck everything away now.'

'Well, you've got to get up there and go through it all before he does!' She nudged me excitedly. 'It's dead thrilling, isn't it? I'm really glad you started telling me about it.'

'Dead thrilling for you, maybe.'

I showed her some of the rest of the photographs and she said that Melanie looked fun.

I looked at the photograph of Melanie at the zoo, pointing at the sign by Chi Chi's cage and smiling. She did look a laugh.

It was strange; I'd started off by hardly knowing or caring whether Melanie had existed or not, then I'd passed through a brief spell of resenting her, and now she was more real to me than she'd ever been. I actually felt that I missed her, which was weird, because how can you miss someone you've never known?

There was a sudden crash as the outer doors of the sixth-form block opened, banged against the wall, and Sara and a bunch of her cronies came in giggling together about something.

Nicki handed the photographs back to me and I tucked them into a folder.

'You missed the disco, then!' Sara called across to me.

I nodded carelessly, as if missing discos was nothing to me. 'It was fantastic!' she said. 'What a laugh! That Jacko's a scream, you know!'

'You were going, weren't you?' Nicki interrupted. 'I thought Jacko asked you, Jo?'

I nodded, grateful to her. 'I was. My father wouldn't let me, though.'

Sara let out a shriek. 'Whose father nowadays doesn't let them out to a disco?!'

'Jo's, obviously,' Nicki said dryly. 'Still, I expect it was nice to be asked.'

'The DJ they had was absolutely useless so Jacko took the whole thing over!' Sara said. 'Still, I expect he's told you, has he?'

'Not yet.'

'Mind you!' she added, 'he didn't take over until he'd had practically every slow dance with Danielle. You couldn't tear them away from each other.'

She looked at me spitefully. 'I don't suppose he'll tell you *that* bit.'

Nicki linked her arm through mine. 'Come over and look at my French revision, will you? I've gone wrong somewhere down the list of tenses and I can't see where.'

I went, relieved to get away, but knowing that Sara would always be able to get at me about Jacko because of the way things were between me and him. It was a funny situation: I didn't know whether I was going out with him or not. How could I say I was going out with someone when I wasn't allowed out?

After school there was a brief meeting with Mrs Salter about the trip to France. We were told the sort of things we'd have to take with us and it was emphasized that it wasn't a holiday, so although we were going to a spa town in Normandy we weren't going to be lazing about and enjoying ourselves.

'You must remember that you are still in school time and this is a major part of your "A" level,' Mrs Salter said, 'so there won't be any trips out or disappearing to dances in the evenings.'

I nodded. I didn't care how hard I had to work when I got there, for me it would be six days away from home – six days of bliss. I'd never been abroad before – none of my family had.

'We'll arrange for your insurance,' Mrs Salter said, 'but you must get your own Form E111 from the Department of Health and Social Security, and make sure that your passport is in order. Those of you who haven't got a current passport can take one of these forms and get it filled in by their parents tonight.'

I leant over and picked up a form from the desk. My own passport . . . once I had one I'd be able to get away, escape from home, whenever I wanted.

'School uniform at all times, of course,' she went on, and everyone groaned.

'Not school uniform in the evenings!' Emma said.

Mrs Salter softened a little. 'In the evenings you will be allowed to wear your own clothes. With discretion, though, girls! No torn jeans or stilettos, please.

'There's a letter and form here for your parents to fill in – and they'll be invited to a presentation evening at the end of the month,' Mrs Salter said. 'They'll be able to look at the work done by the girls who went to Normandy last year.'

I went out clutching my papers. The trip was at the end of November so there wasn't very long to get everything arranged, and as I didn't have a passport I'd have to get my father to fill in that form quickly.

I was thrilled when I found Jacko was waiting outside school for me.

'I thought I'd missed you!' he said, smiling as I approached. 'I got out of my class especially early, too.'

We walked towards the bus stop and I told him about the French meeting and then, even though I was dying to tell him about the things I'd found in Melanie's box, I just had to ask him about the disco.

'It was okay,' he shrugged. 'Pretty mediocre as discos go, actually.'

I eyed him a bit jealously. 'I heard you were the life and soul ... Sara said that you took over the DJ's spot.'

'Only for half an hour while he went home for a load of records he'd forgotten.' He took my hand. 'Sara was just trying to make it sound good because you weren't there.'

I nodded. 'I know.' We reached the bus stop and, because there were quite a few people waiting, decided to walk on to the next one so that we could talk.

'She also said you and Danielle were locked in each other's arms all night!' I said, trying to make my voice sound mocking.

'That girl's nose will start growing!' Jacko said. 'I did have a dance with Danielle – but only because she came up and asked me. Pestered me, actually.'

'I expect she fancies you,' I said lightly.

He shook his head. 'They're taking the mickey,' he said. 'They like anything in trousers, those two.' He squeezed my hand. 'Anyway, who cares about them – what sort of a weekend did you have? How was the ogre?'

'Just wait till you hear this!' I said, and I told him all that had happened: about all the things I'd found in the box and also what Nicki had said. 'And just look at the photos!' I added when I'd finished, and I fished some of them out of the file I was carrying.

He looked at them for a while, sorting backwards and forwards through them and whistling under his breath in an appreciative sort of way.

'I think it's her I should be asking to discos!' he said when he handed them back to me. I gave him a push.

'You know what I mean, though. I bet your father had some trouble trying to tie *her* down.'

'I don't think he ever managed it,' I said, 'that's why he's never given me an inch of freedom – in case I took a mile, like Melanie obviously did.'

We reached the next bus stop just as the bus came round the corner.

'Just suppose she's still alive. . .' I said.

He nodded. 'I already thought of that when you first told me about her.'

'Nicki – well, *she* thinks that there might have been

a tremendous row and my father just chucked her out.'

'So what are we waiting for? Now that I've seen a photo of her I'm all for finding her.'

'She wouldn't look like that now! She'd be about thirty-two.'

'The older woman, eh? I've always fancied being a toy boy.'

I pretended to be cross, but I didn't really mind him teasing me. For one thing, I couldn't really believe that Melanie was alive. I would have had some clue about it before now, surely; someone would have said something. But then there wasn't anyone to say anything ... no aunties or uncles, no cousins. Mum had friends at the Oxfam shop but she never saw them outside – and in any case, they were all quite new friends. There were no old friends or neighbours who had known us when Melanie was around. Why was that? Was it just the way things had happened, or had my parents deliberately engineered it to be that way?

I was sure of one thing, though: whatever had happened sixteen years ago, I was going to get to the bottom of it. Now that I'd started, and now that I had Jacko to help me, I was going to carry on to the end.

Chapter 9

Melanie . . . I couldn't stop thinking about her. I lay on my bed and went through the photographs again, looking for clues, background . . . something which would give me a firmer hold on her. I looked at the faces of her friends: they must still be around; they'd know what had happened to her. Where would I find them, though? I could hardly go round the streets putting up WANTED posters with their photographs on them. Anyway, they'd all be older now, look totally different . . . just as Melanie would if she was still alive. I held up the zoo photograph and stared at it: it was difficult to imagine her any other way than the way she was there. To think that if she was alive and I passed her in the street, I might not recognize her.

There was a noise outside in the hall and then Mum popped her head round my bedroom door. I swiftly pushed the photographs under some of the clutter of homework on my bed.

'Dinner's nearly ready, dear,' she said.

'OK. I'm just coming. She went out and I suddenly thought of something. 'Mum!' I called.

'What, dear?' Her voice came from the top of the stairs.

'I want to ask Dad to fill in the form tonight giving permission for the trip to France. He will let me go, won't he?'

She came back again, stood in the doorway. 'I should think so,' she said. 'He's always for anything which might help your education, and as long as he's satisfied that you're going to be properly supervised out there.'

I nodded. 'And Mum,' I added quickly, before she went away again, 'I'm sorry you got upset on Saturday. I didn't mean you to come in and see me dressed like that.'

'Let's say no more about it, Jo.'

'But I just wanted...'

'No more,' she said firmly. Surprisingly firmly for her. She made a gesture towards downstairs; 'There's your father's key in the lock. You don't want him to hear you talking about all that sort of thing and get on the wrong side of him if you're going to ask a favour, do you?'

'No, Mum.' I said resignedly. I'd been hoping to ask her about where we used to live, but obviously I couldn't now.

I tidied some of the stuff on my bed and stowed the photographs away underneath; I'd prised a corner of the carpet up just there and they tucked in nicely. It was funny how devious I was getting – and it was also funny how gradually, very gradually, I was getting less scared of my father. Even six months ago I wouldn't have dreamt of rebelling, even slightly, much less discussed him as 'the ogre' with someone outside the family.

I went downstairs, Grace was said and dinner went on as usual with my mother and father making polite conversation about their day as if they were strangers getting to know each other. I waited until we'd washed up and Dad was in the sitting room with the newspaper and a cup of coffee, then took the necessary papers concerning the trip to France in to him.

'Mrs Salter has sent this form home to be filled in,' I said politely. 'You did say I could go to France, didn't you?'

'I don't see why not,' he said, and he put his newspaper down, adjusted his glasses and started to read carefully through the small print: all about how our time would be spent and the insurance details and arrangements for giving out spending money.

'Where's the sum payable?' he asked after a moment.

I pointed to the box at the bottom. 'Although as it's to do with our "A" levels, Mrs Salter says that most of it will be recoverable from the local authorities.'

He nodded gravely. 'And do you have to have any special vaccinations or anything?'

'No, Dad,' I said, 'not for France. 'It's only just across the Channel.'

'And what about currency and so on?'

'Mrs Salter is arranging to get our spending money changed for us.'

'And are there reciprocal health arrangements with France?'

I stifled a sigh. 'There are, but there'll also be a group insurance. It's all organized very carefully, Dad. They go every year.'

'Quite. Quite.'

Mum came in from the kitchen and nodded meaningfully at me as if to say so far, so good.

'Soon there'll be a special showing of the work done by last year's group,' I said as he started to fill in the form. 'Being actually in the country really improves everyone's accent, you know.'

I thought about other plus-points I could mention; I just wanted him to keep filling that form in and get to his signature at the bottom. 'Shall I get your cheque book for the deposit?' I asked. 'It's only £20 but we've got to pay it by the end of the week.'

He stopped filling the form in, frowned. 'It says here something about a passport.'

'It's another fifteen pounds but it lasts for ten years. Some of them are getting a British visitors' passport but. . .'

'I thought you'd just give your names and all go under the care of the teacher in charge.'

'Yes, but we can't if we're over sixteen,' I said patiently. 'We've each got to have our own passport.'

'But you. . .' He was looking agitated, I couldn't think why – unless it was the cost of it all.

'If it's the money, I'll pay the fifteen pounds. I've still got some of my birthday money left.'

He still didn't say anything. Mum hadn't sat down, but was standing by the mantelpiece fidgeting with the little china figures.

'Here's the form, here.' I held it up and read out the details. 'There's nothing much to it. You've just got to have three photographs – I'll get them done in a booth, that's no problem – one of which has to be signed by a teacher or someone, this form filled in and your birth certificate.'

As I said the last word a look flashed between my father and mother, then Mum put down one of the China figures with a sharp noise and, looking agitated, hurried back into the kitchen.

'What's up?' I said, amazed. 'Why can't I have a passport of my own?'

'It's not that,' my father said.

'Do you think I'm going to run away or something, is that it?'

He didn't say anything, just stared at the form.

'Everyone else is going to have one ... why have I got to be different again?' I pushed the form at him, on the verge of tears. 'I've got to have a passport or I can't go!'

'I'm afraid you won't be able to go, then.'

'But *why?*!'

'Several reasons.'

My lower lip trembled. 'Give me one of them!'

He folded the form carefully and tried to give it back to me but I wouldn't take it and it fluttered to the floor.

'I do not have to give reasons,' he said, looking at me over his glasses. 'If I say you're not going, then you're not.'

'You do have to give me a reason!' I cried. 'It's not fair. You said I could go...'

'And now I say you can't.'

I burst into tears. 'You ... you...'

'I would remind you that while you're under my roof you do as I say.' He pushed his glasses back and, picking up the newspaper, seemed to indicate that the conversation was closed.

'You're just being unreasonable. There's no reason why I...' I hesitated. 'You think I'm going to run away, don't you? Is that what Melanie did? Did she go abroad to get away from you? Well, I don't blame her and as soon as I can go – I will!'

I knew I sounded childish, but I didn't care, I just

wanted to provoke some reaction from him. He just sat there, though, with his stupid old-fashioned round glasses and his ridiculous wispy hair and his nasty little thin lips pursed, and he didn't say a thing.

'You . . . you're pathetic!' I burst out, 'D'you know that? Completely pathetic!'

'I think you'd better go to your room, Joanna,' he said.

'That's your answer to everything, isn't it?' I said bitterly. 'As soon as there's something which you don't want to face, you send me to my room.'

'I'll write to Mrs Salter and tell her that you won't be going on the trip.'

'I'm going to find out about Melanie, you know.' I said, my voice trembling. 'You think you've got everything hidden away, but I'm going to find out. I know there's a secret,' I blustered. Now I'd started I had to carry on. 'I know there's something you want to hide – something awful which no one is allowed to talk about!'

He said absolutely nothing, just folded the newspaper carefully so that the crossword was uppermost and reached into his pocket for a pen.

'You're a pig! A hateful pig!' That may not sound very strong, but when you've never dared raise your voice to your father before it's strong enough and just saying it near enough frightened me to death. I didn't dare wait to see what the reaction was, just ran out of the room as soon as I'd spoken.

I flung myself on my bed, trembling all over. This was it, really it. I'd had enough. If I'd had the smallest scruples before about going behind my father's back, I certainly didn't have now. He *was* a pig. How could Mum have stayed with him all these years? How,

'What's up?' I said, amazed. 'Why can't I have a passport of my own?'

'It's not that,' my father said.

'Do you think I'm going to run away or something, is that it?'

He didn't say anything, just stared at the form.

'Everyone else is going to have one . . . why have I got to be different again?' I pushed the form at him, on the verge of tears. 'I've got to have a passport or I can't go!'

'I'm afraid you won't be able to go, then.'

'But *why?*!'

'Several reasons.'

My lower lip trembled. 'Give me one of them!'

He folded the form carefully and tried to give it back to me but I wouldn't take it and it fluttered to the floor.

'I do not have to give reasons,' he said, looking at me over his glasses. 'If I say you're not going, then you're not.'

'You do have to give me a reason!' I cried. 'It's not fair. You said I could go. . .'

'And now I say you can't.'

I burst into tears. 'You . . . you. . .'

'I would remind you that while you're under my roof you do as I say.' He pushed his glasses back and, picking up the newspaper, seemed to indicate that the conversation was closed.

'You're just being unreasonable. There's no reason why I. . .' I hesitated. 'You think I'm going to run away, don't you? Is that what Melanie did? Did she go abroad to get away from you? Well, I don't blame her and as soon as I can go – I will!'

I knew I sounded childish, but I didn't care, I just

wanted to provoke some reaction from him. He just sat there, though, with his stupid old-fashioned round glasses and his ridiculous wispy hair and his nasty little thin lips pursed, and he didn't say a thing.

'You . . . you're pathetic!' I burst out, 'D'you know that? Completely pathetic!'

'I think you'd better go to your room, Joanna,' he said.

'That's your answer to everything, isn't it?' I said bitterly. 'As soon as there's something which you don't want to face, you send me to my room.'

'I'll write to Mrs Salter and tell her that you won't be going on the trip.'

'I'm going to find out about Melanie, you know.' I said, my voice trembling. 'You think you've got everything hidden away, but I'm going to find out. I know there's a secret,' I blustered. Now I'd started I had to carry on. 'I know there's something you want to hide – something awful which no one is allowed to talk about!'

He said absolutely nothing, just folded the newspaper carefully so that the crossword was uppermost and reached into his pocket for a pen.

'You're a pig! A hateful pig!' That may not sound very strong, but when you've never dared raise your voice to your father before it's strong enough and just saying it near enough frightened me to death. I didn't dare wait to see what the reaction was, just ran out of the room as soon as I'd spoken.

I flung myself on my bed, trembling all over. This was it, really it. I'd had enough. If I'd had the smallest scruples before about going behind my father's back, I certainly didn't have now. He *was* a pig. How could Mum have stayed with him all these years? How, even, could I have put up with sixteen years of it? Only because there hadn't been any alternative, I suppose, because I'd been so totally subservient that it hadn't occurred to me to question things, to wonder what would happen if he was ever crossed – to even think that he *could* be crossed without the end of the world coming.

I suddenly leant across my bed, pulled up the piece of carpet and got out the photographs of Melanie. I then walked to my notice board, took down all the notices from school and reminders about my 'A' levels, and carefully pinned up the photographs of Melanie and her friends instead. All over it.

I was sorry about Mum; I knew she'd get upset when she saw them, but it was my way of asserting my independence. They didn't want me to know anything about Melanie, they didn't want to acknowledge her, but I was going to force them into it. Whatever happened, I was going to change things.

Chapter 10

'Well, I must say, Joanna, it seems very hard on you that you can't go to France.' Mrs Salter said. 'Do you think it would do any good if I had a talk to your parents?'

I shook my head miserably. 'It was OK when my father thought we were going on a collective passport, but then he found out I had to have one of my own and just went all peculiar and said I couldn't go.'

Mrs Salter frowned. 'How strange. I mean, it's not for me to question the ideas of parents but I do think. . .' She hesitated. 'I remember your parents at interview evenings; they're very much older than our other parents, aren't they?'

I nodded.

'Perhaps that's it. Your father thinks you're going to rush off somewhere; maybe he can't come to terms with the sort of freedom young women have today.'

I made a face. 'There's not a lot of freedom in *our* house.'

'Would you like me to come round? I'm sure I could persuade him. He's very keen for you to get good marks, isn't he? How would it be if I emphasized the benefits to be gained by living for a few days in a foreign country and speaking the native tongue.'

'I wouldn't bother,' I said, then added quickly, 'I

mean, thanks all the same but it wouldn't do any good. It would probably put his back up even more.'

'But you're one of our most promising pupils,' she said, shaking her head. 'I do hope this isn't going to put you off taking your French exam.'

'It won't,' I said. Once I had *that*, I'd be eighteen and then he couldn't stop me leaving home. I could go abroad: get a job as an au pair in France.

'And you say it was only getting a passport of your own he objected to?' Mrs Salter said thoughtfully.

I nodded. 'I can't think of another reason. He was actually filling in the form – and then he just suddenly changed his mind.'

She looked at me for a moment, as if sizing me up. 'I hope you won't mind me asking you this, Joanna, but have you got a birth certificate?'

I stared at her. 'I suppose I have.'

'Have you ever seen it?'

'Well, no, I don't think so. But I mean, everyone has a birth certificate, don't they?'

'Not always. Sometimes they have to apply for one.'

I shook my head. 'I don't see what you're getting at.'

'Maybe . . . maybe your father didn't want to apply for one.' She suddenly patted me on the arm. 'Look, don't worry, Joanna. I shouldn't be delving into all this; it's really none of my business and if your father found out that I was questioning you about your family affairs I don't think he'd like it very much.' The bell signalling the start of the first lesson went and she picked up a pile of books from her desk. 'Sorry, I'll have to go,' she said, 'I've got to get over to the English block.'

I shook my head, still puzzled.

'All I can say is — if I can do anything to help or if you want to talk about your situation at home, let me know,' she said, ushering me out.

I felt miserable all the rest of that day. I was tired, my eyes were itchy from having cried the night before, and Sara kept having a go at me. I knew I should have answered her back, I knew I was being rabbity, but that day I just didn't have the guts to speak up to her. I hadn't seen Jacko that morning, either, or he might have given me a bit of a boost. Dad had been late going to work and because I'd stayed upstairs to keep out of his way, I'd missed the usual bus.

I half thought Jacko might be waiting outside school for me that evening, but he wasn't, which almost threw me into an even greater depression, but just as I was going out of the gates a girl in jeans and a pink sweatshirt came up to me; a girl I'd never seen before.

'Are you Jo?' she asked.

I nodded.

'I recognized you from Jacko's description!' she said, and I looked at her a bit warily: it didn't seem to be my day and for all I knew she could be Danielle come to have a go at me. 'I'm at Greatlands with him,' she went on, 'I've come to meet my younger sister — she's here in your first year.'

I smiled at her, she seemed okay. She pulled something out of her pocket.

'Jacko said to give you this note,' she said, 'he's got to stay late to watch *King Lear* or something.' She handed over a folded piece of paper and I took it and thanked her.

'There's my sister!' she said, waving towards a little blonde first year, 'I've got to get her to the dentist,' and then she said 'See you!' to me and rushed over to her.

I called my thanks and unfolded the note.

'Hi, Jo!' it said,

'I missed you this morning and I've got to stay late now. Are you allowed to the library? It's open until nine tonight; I could meet you there from about seven onwards. If you can, I'll see you in the record library section (it's not so busy). Have you got any news?

Love, Jacko.'

My depression lifted immediately and I read it over and over again on the bus going home. My first letter from a boy. OK, it wasn't exactly a love letter, but at least it showed he was thinking about me.

I started to plan how I could get out. I'd never been to the library before in the evening — we had a good library at school which always had everything I needed — but who was to say that I wasn't doing a special project that needed some extra reference books?

I got it all worked out and mentioned it when we were sitting down for dinner at regulation time.

'Can you let me off the washing-up tonight?' I asked Mum, 'I've got this special project I'm working on at school and I can't find the right books in our library. I want to pop into town for an hour or so.'

'Of course, dear,' she said, 'I can manage quite well on my own.' She smiled at me a bit anxiously; I knew she was trying to make up for the fact that I wasn't going to France.

I ate my food with one eye on the clock: my father

seemed to eat deliberately slowly, asking for another potato and then wanting extra gravy made up. Finally, at five to seven and half dying of impatience, I was released from the table and dashed upstairs to get changed.

I shuffled through the things hanging in my wardrobe. I didn't really know why, because I knew everything that was in there; no wonderful trendy items had suddenly appeared overnight. I hunted through them all the same, though, and finally decided that jeans were the safest bet. I put those on with a fairly decent bright red jumper that I'd bought with my birthday money, and finally, in an effort to make myself look completely different, held my head down and brushed my hair until it was in a high pony tail on the top. That would have to do.

When I got to the library Jacko was sitting on the window seat thumbing through the catalogue – or pretending to. He looked up when I pushed the swing doors open and our eyes locked as I crossed the room so that I couldn't look away. I sat down beside him, my heart thumping.

'You look nice,' he said, 'I like your hair like that.'

'Thanks.' I was still looking at him; I felt as if I never wanted to stop.

'OK?' he asked. 'Did you have trouble getting out?'

I shook my head. 'It was easy. He *might* have objected but then he's not talking to me, so it was a bit difficult.'

'Why's that then?'

I told him about the night before and the fuss about the trip to France. 'It ended up with me calling him a pig and running off to my room,' I said. 'For that he probably won't ever speak to me again.'

'That's his loss, then,' Jacko said, 'Don't worry about it. I mean who wants to talk to an ogre anyway?' He smiled at me and edged a little closer on the window seat. It was nice in the library; warm and secluded. We couldn't be seen from the desk and the only two customers there were flicking through LPs on the racks and not even glancing at us. I felt a terrible urge to touch him, felt myself melting where he was leaning against me.

'I miss you when I don't see you in the mornings,' he said. 'I've got used to you cheering up my days.'

'You don't need me to cheer you up – you always have a laugh at Greatlands,' I said. 'It's not like my school.'

'Yeah, it's not bad. You're not there, though,' he added meaningfully.

I stared into his eyes. The atmosphere had suddenly got heavy and I was having awful difficulty breathing. I struggled to think of something to say, something normal. 'That . . . that girl who brought me the note was nice. Is she in the crowd you go round with?'

He moved closer still. 'Who wants to talk about her?' His arm slid round my shoulders. 'Jo,' he said, 'this probably isn't the time or the place, but. . .'

Jo . . . it was the way he'd said my name. My heart started doing overtime again and my mouth went dry.

His hand traced a line down the side of my cheek and I went trembly all over. I closed my eyes as he kissed me and when I opened them again everything had taken on a dreamy quality: as if the world had shifted very slightly out of focus.

'I've been waiting to do that since – oh, some day way back in September when I first saw you at the bus stop,' he whispered, and I just smiled back at him dizzily.

It was wonderful. He didn't kiss me again but we stayed there for ages just talking about everything: about life and feelings and all the things I had no one else to talk to about. When the bell went to say that the library was about to close I couldn't believe how late it was.

We parted on the library steps. I didn't think my father would walk down to meet me but I didn't want to take any risks and have him spoil what had turned out to be a magic evening.

Jacko took my hand and held it tightly. 'I'll see you in the morning,' he said, 'and don't forget you've got to try and get up in the loft as soon as you can. The minute we get an address or something...'

I nodded and said I would. It was Mum's afternoon at the Oxfam shop the following day, so if I got home from school quickly I might have a chance.

He kissed me again and I walked home feeling blissful. OK, my home life was a drag but having Jacko made up for everything. I could even bear living with an ogre as long as I had Jacko...

Chapter 11

I let myself in our front door.

'Hello, Mum!' I called, and as I expected there was no reply. I dumped my school bag on the floor and raced up the stairs, throwing my cloak over the bannisters as I ran. I had ten minutes or so before Mum got in. Ten minutes to get in the loft and to gather as much information as I could.

That morning on the bus Jacko had said not to mess about searching through everything, just to grab up as much paperwork as I could and go back down to my room with it. He was scared that I'd get caught up there again.

I made my way across the loft by walking along one of the roof beams. I couldn't find the torch and the light from the hall scarcely reached the tea chest where Melanie's things were so I had to feel rather than see what I was doing. My fingers touched scratchy plywood and I pushed into the tea chest past the LPs and the clothes and the pop posters and towards where I'd seen some letters and papers. Underneath almost everything else was a largish cardboard box with a tattered satin bow stretched across it, looking as if it had once contained chocolates. The lid didn't fit on properly and there were things falling out: letters and exercise books and odd scraps of paper with notes on, but they were just the sort of things I was looking for, so I grabbed up the whole box, stuffing things back inside the lid as best I could.

I was all of a jitter by then in case Mum came back, so I made my way back to the ladder, more or less threw the box down, then climbed down myself, putting the hatch back in position on my way.

I took the box inside my bedroom, closed the door and just stared at it, almost frightened to lift the lid and start looking. This might be *it*, in this box – the answer to all the questions – the reason why Dad was like he was, the truth about what had happened to Melanie. Once I'd looked into it, everything might become clear.

I stared up at the photographs on my notice board – the ones of Melanie and her friends: was I really going to find out what had happened to her? I felt like one of those investigative reporters that you get on the TV prying into people's business and putting things right.

I knew I mustn't leave the box in the middle of my bedroom floor though, it had to be hidden somewhere safe, and just as I thought that, I heard Mum come in the front door and call up the stairs for me. I was pretty sure she wouldn't actually come up so I just called to her that I was in, had loads of homework and I'd be down later.

I pushed the chocolate box into the bottom of my wardrobe under two pairs of old wellington boots. I'd take it slowly, I decided, just take out one thing at a time. If I found anything really exciting I had to ring Jacko so that he could meet me down at the library. He'd said that if there was anything sensational, then he wanted to know about it straight away.

I took a deep breath, pushed my hand into the box and pulled out a school rough book similar to the ones we used – except this one had 'Kent County Council' printed on it, and ours had Surrey. This was a clue already: now I knew the county where we used to live. 'Melanie McIver' was written on the front with little drawings all round it. I began to turn the pages slowly.

Melanie's handwriting was scrawly, careless – not like mine was. I smiled as I turned the pages and Melanie began to come alive again for me: there were the usual sorts of things you get in a school rough book – notes about homework, recipes given out in Home Economics – but also little notes to friends, scraps of songs, two or three lines of a poem, silly drawings, a page headed 'Top Ten favourite boys'. This had only one name on it: 'Sam Booker', it said, written ten times all down the page. I glanced up to the photographs again: that was his name, then: the boy Melanie was always with. He must be Sam.

I sat on the floor deep in thought, totally preoccupied, thinking about Melanie and Sam – had she felt about him, I wondered, the way I felt about Jacko? – and didn't hear my bedroom door open.

'I thought you had loads of homework!' Mum said.

I jumped guiltily, put my hand over the book. 'I have.'

'Then how is it you've left all your school books downstairs in this bag?' she asked, swinging my school bag through the door.

'I . . . er . . . haven't started today's homework yet,' I said, 'I'm still doing yesterday's. I'm . . . er . . . reading through my notes.'

'Well, the books are here when you want them.'

She stood in the doorway, obviously wanting to chat. 'Anything you want? Would you like a snack to keep you going?'

'No thanks.'

She hesitated and then she went out. I stared at the door after she'd closed it. Poor old Mum; she was so much under my father's thumb, so programmed to live exactly by his rulebook that she'd never be able to live any other sort of way. I shook my head sadly, feeling sorry for her. I had a chance to change, but she'd never be able to.

I turned back to the rough book again, reading right through it from beginning to end and laughing at some of the things Melanie had written, and then I put it to one side and picked up a pile of letters all addressed to her. I flicked through them, there were all sorts: a bank statement; her National Insurance card; some postcards from friends on holiday; some fattish letters written in blue ink all in the same handwriting; a library reminder; a couple of letters from someone in Devon. It seemed to be just as I'd thought before: as if Mum had scooped up the contents of her bedroom and put them on ice. It was understandable, I suppose; if she *had* died, Mum wouldn't want constant reminders about the place – and probably it had seemed callous to Mum to just throw everything away and pretend Melanie had never existed – though I bet my father had wanted her to do just that.

I stared at the letters excitedly. There was one thing they all had in common, and this was my best discovery to date: they all had the same address written on the envelopes!

'24 Wychwood Road, Burnley, Kent,' I murmured

to myself, and knew I wouldn't have to write it down to remember it. So now I knew where once upon a time we'd all lived, and Jacko and I could go back there and ask questions.

I started to look at the fat blue letters, but they were love letters – from Sam – and I didn't like to read them. Whether she was dead or alive I didn't think she'd like anyone reading her really private things. There were quite a few of them, though, and it was obvious from the little I already knew of her that Sam had been the only boy in her life. It was typical of my father, then, whenever he referred to her, always to give the impression that she'd had loads of boyfriends; had run wild with a whole pack of them.

I put the letters to one side, delved in to see what else I could find. There were two diaries, one for 1971 and one for 1972, filled with three- or four-word entries like 'Get project in' and 'Meet Sam 7.00'. There were also other odd messages: 'Mum's birthday, get flowers' and two or three references to my father: 'Row with dad' and 'Dad ... what an oaf!' I loved reading those; to know that Melanie hadn't got on with him either made me feel great. I felt she would approve of what I was doing now. There was also, in October 1971, one entry which was indecipherable because it had been scribbled all over with a thick black felt tip pen. Underneath, on the next date, there was an arrow pointing to the black square and, written in pencil: 'This was the worst day of my life'.

I tried to, but I couldn't read what had originally been written, though I absolutely ached to know. As I was holding it up to the light, though, my attention was caught by something else in the box, something that looked like a birthday card, folded over and separate from the other things, as if it had been stuffed down the side of the cardboard box as an afterthought.

I flattened it out; it was a cheapish-looking envelope, going slightly brown at the edges, addressed to 'Miss Susanna McIver' at the old address. Someone had re-addressed it, crossing out Wychwood Road and putting our present address in.

Susanna McIver. I frowned ... I'd never heard of anyone in the family called Susanna. I opened it and pulled out the card inside. To my surprise it was a baby's first birthday card: a big pink teddy with a bow round his neck made of real ribbon which had been pink once but was now faded to a dull white.

I opened it and recognized Melanie's scrawly handwriting straight away. It wasn't that which made me draw in my breath with a startled gasp, though; it was what had been written by her under the printed poem:

'To my darling Susanna, with love from her Mummy. I'll always be thinking of you, darling.'

A baby! Melanie had had a baby! So *that* was what had happened; *that* was why my father was so strict with me. But where was the baby, though? What had they done with Susanna?

Chapter 12

'It'll be OK; don't worry,' Jacko said, squeezing my hand.

'Suppose we find out something dreadful,' I shivered. It was Saturday and we were on the train to London. We had to go up to the mainline station, cross on the underground and go out to Kent: to Wychwood Road, Burnley, Kent.

'Are you cold?' Jacko asked, and he put his arm round me tightly.

I shivered again. 'Cold and scared,' I said, but I pressed my nose into the warmth of his padded skiing jacket and felt a bit better. It seemed to me like he was the only steady thing in the world; the only person I could rely on.

'D'you want to put my coat on?'

I shook my head. 'I'd rather cuddle it on you.'

He grinned. 'Well, don't let me stop you.'

I put my arm around his waist, rested my head on his shoulder. 'I just couldn't believe it when I saw the card. A baby! Fancy them keeping it quiet all these years.'

He nodded. 'At least we know something definite about her now, though, don't we?'

'Yes, but what happened to it?'

'That's what we've got to find out.

'Well, suppose we don't find out anything over there? Suppose no one remembers my family?'

'Then it's back to the drawing board. We'll look up old newspapers ... contact Social Security with the number on her card. There are loads of different things we can try now that we know more about her.'

I began to feel better; Jacko usually had that effect on me. When he was around things never seemed so scary or so impossible.

'How did you manage to get out this morning, then?' he asked.

'I made up a complete and utter lie. I told my father that there was a day trip to do with the Normandy visit and they were going to the French National Tourist Office and then visiting a French school for the afternoon.'

'You're getting devious!' Jacko said. 'It must be my influence. I'm still surprised he let you out, though.'

'I was really clever about how I did it – I played it very hurt and martyred. I said that Mrs Salter had specifically asked for me to go, seeing as I was missing the trip to Normandy, but of course if he wasn't going to let me go today either...'

'And what did he say to that?'

'Not a lot. He's still not really talking to me. Mum spoke up for once, though – said that she thought I ought to go and that even a day doing French sort of things might help my 'A' levels. Mum's okay really,' I said thoughtfully. 'I just wish she'd stand up for herself. Dad seems to have some sort of hold over her; when he's around, her personality undergoes a change. She becomes all browbeaten and submissive.'

'Quite right,' Jacko said, 'that's how women ought to be.'

I dug my fingers into his ribs and he curled up laughing.

I sat and watched the scenery flash by. It had rained a lot recently and the rivers were swollen and fields flooded. The cows were knee-deep in water and horses stood impassively staring over fences, their coats sodden.

'What will we do when we find out?' I asked suddenly.

'That depends on what we find, doesn't it? Maybe it's a whole lot simpler than we thought,' Jacko said. 'Maybe she found she was having a baby and when she told your father he just hit the roof and chucked her out, would have nothing more to do with her. Strict parents did things like that years ago, didn't they?'

'I don't know about years ago,' I said. 'My father would be like that today.'

'And perhaps Melanie went off somewhere – to a mother and baby home or something – to have the baby, and then she never darkened their doors again.'

'Yes, but. . .' I could see a flaw there somewhere – and then realized what it was. 'OK, she went off somewhere and they never saw her again – but then why would she send a baby card to our old address?'

Jacko looked thoughtful. 'Yeah. That's a point.'

It started raining again. Hard, so that it fell against the windows in great diagonal streaks.

'Maybe this accident when she died – this motor-bike accident or whatever it was – happened after she'd had the baby,' Jacko suggested.

'But we've still got the problem of the baby – where did it go?'

Jacko shook his head.

It was still raining when we crossed London, but had steadied to a fine drizzle by the time we came out of Burnley Station. I felt scared and shivery again by then – and conspicuous, too – as if someone might recognize me in the street, point a finger at me and shout 'Look – there's a member of that notorious McIver family!'

Of course, no such thing happened. Jacko went into a newsagent's to buy a map of the area and we found Wychwood Road on it and started to walk there. Neither of us were speaking much by this time, but Jacko held my hand tightly and occasionally said something silly to try and make me laugh.

The area was a typical suburb: semi-detached houses, tree-lined streets and neat gardens. It took half an hour of walking before we got to Wychwood Road, and when we reached it we just stood there at the top and looked at each other.

'I'm dead scared of the next bit,' I faltered. 'I don't want to go any further.'

'Well, I do! If you like, you stay here and I'll go and do the asking.'

I shook my head and leant against him. 'I've got to do it myself. I just want a minute or two to think about what I'm going to say.'

He put his arms tightly round me. 'Courage, mon amie!' he said in a ludicrous French accent. 'You must 'ave ze so-called guts.' He looked up the road, 'Hang on here a sec,' he said, 'we just passed a corner shop. I'll go and get us something to eat. Maybe your blood sugar level's low.' He grinned, 'See – we've done all that Biology business at school, too.'

'I couldn't eat a thing!' I wailed, but he ran off

and came back a couple of minutes later with a bar of chocolate and I did manage to eat a few squares.

We walked down to number 24. I hesitated outside, looking up at the net-curtained windows and the shiny red front door. There were dead or resting rose bushes all along the front edge to the garden; had my father put them in, looked after them once? It was funny, but I didn't feel a thing: no pang of recognition, no stirring of faint memory, as I'd thought I would have done. I'd once lived in this house. At least, that was what I'd always been told – but then, I'd been told so many things.

'There's no stopping now!' Jacko said, and, pulling me with him, he pushed open the white-painted gate and marched straight up the path.

When the door was opened my heart sank immediately: it was a youngish woman with a child in her arms and I felt sure she couldn't possibly know anything.

Jacko nudged me to speak.

'Er . . . I hope you won't mind us . . . er . . . calling,' I said hesitantly, 'but my family used to live in this house once and I wondered if you could tell me anything about them.'

She looked at me blankly. 'Our name is McIver,' I went on. 'It was quite a few years ago – sixteen or so.'

She shook her head. 'Sorry,' she said, 'we've only been living here two years. Since I had her,' she nodded towards the toddler.

'Did you . . . can you remember where the people went who lived here before?'

'Ooh, somewhere foreign,' she said, 'but they'd only been living here a while as well. I know that because they intended to stay longer – they had the garage built – but then they had to go overseas with his job.'

'Has anyone roundabout been living here since about 1972?' Jacko asked. 'Someone older, perhaps.'

The woman shook her head. 'There aren't many older people about – it's not that sort of place. Everyone's constantly moving on, changing jobs or going to bigger houses.'

'I see,' Jacko said. 'Well, thanks very much, anyway.'

She began to shut the door. 'You could try Mrs Terry over at number 35,' she called just before the door closed, 'she's been here a while.'

I felt gloomy as we walked back down her path. 'Now, you're not to be discouraged,' Jacko said, 'it's early days. You didn't really expect to hit the jackpot first time, did you?'

I nodded slowly. 'I think I did. I had the idea that I'd just knock on the door of our old house and everything would be sitting there waiting to be revealed to me.'

'Maybe this Mrs Terry person will be the one,' Jacko said as we crossed the road to number 35. This was identical to number 24 in every way right down to the same net curtains, but with the addition of a white cat sitting in the window.

Mrs Terry was out. We rang and rang while the cat just sat there and looked at us impassively and the fine rain fell on us.

'We'll try next door,' Jacko said. 'We'll try every house in the blasted road if we have to.'

We tried number 37, but this was also a young mum who'd only been there four years. She said she didn't think Mrs Terry had been there that long either: perhaps just a year or so before she'd come herself.

We started making our way along the road: first one side, then the other. With every door we knocked at I got more and more despondent: several people were out or didn't answer, and when we did find someone to speak to they never had anything to tell us. It eventually turned out, after knocking on every door from one end to the other, that eight years was the longest anyone had been living in the road.

I felt tired and near to tears by the time we'd finished at the last house.

'It's OK,' Jacko said, giving me a little shake, 'we'll just move on to our next option.'

'What's that?'

'The local newspaper office.'

'It wouldn't be open on a Saturday,' I said. 'Anyway, wouldn't you have to have an appointment to look in their archives or whatever it is they're called?'

'Well, then . . . we'll try an old people's home or something – they always have long memories. Or . . . or a doctor! Yeah, when your family lived here, they must have consulted doctors.'

'But we won't be able to look through his files. It's against the rules.'

'But he'd be able to tell you some basic facts – like whether your sister actually died or not.'

We began to walk back to the top of Wychwood Road. 'We'll go back in the shop where I bought the chocolate and ask where the nearest doctor's surgery is.' He looked at my miserable face and gave me another little bracing shake. 'It's worth a try!'

'I suppose so,' I said.

We pushed open the door of the shop. It was one of those really old fashioned places that sells everything: tinned stuff, a few fresh vegetables, bread, string and sausages. Goods were piled higgledy-piggledy upon shelves, counters, vegetable racks and the floor.

'More chocolate?' Jacko asked, and I nodded. I felt I needed something.

An oldish woman came from out of the back wearing a shiny blue nylon overall.

'Another large bar of fruit and nut and can you tell me where the nearest doctor's surgery is, please?'

She nodded impassively, turned to get the chocolate and handed it to Jacko. Then she looked at me and her jaw dropped.

'Good Lord,' she said, 'you gave me quite a turn. It's Melanie, isn't it? Well, wherever have you been all these years?'

Chapter 13

'It's not . . . I'm not Melanie,' I whispered.

The woman stared at me. 'Well, I never! Whoever you are, you look just like her, then. Her twin, you could be!'

Jacko gave me a reassuring hug. 'This is Joanna,' he said to the woman. 'She's Melanie's sister.'

She peered at me closely, shook her head. 'Of course . . . now that you say that. Bless me, I'm forgetting myself; I mean, *you* look like Melanie used to twenty or so years ago. She wouldn't look like that now.'

Jacko took command. 'We've been looking for anyone that might have known Melanie and her family. D'you think we could talk to you for a moment, ask you some questions?'

'Well, ask away, dear,' the woman said. 'I don't know as I'll be able to tell you much, though. If I remember rightly, your family was one that kept very much to itself.'

'That sounds like us,' I said wryly.

'You'd better come through to the back.'

We followed the woman through two doors into a tiny room with two chairs pulled up in front of an electric fire. This room was obviously used to store things for the shop, because it was piled high with boxes and cartons.

'You sit yourself down, dear,' the woman said to

me, pointing to one of the chairs. 'You look quite done in.'

I undid my coat and ran my hand through my damp hair. 'I'm okay,' I said, 'It was just a bit of a shock, I think. We've been looking for someone who might have known Melanie all day and I'd just about given up hope.'

She settled herself in the other chair and Jacko came over and leant on the back of mine.

'Well, what can I tell you?' she asked. 'They lived just about halfway up Wychwood Road, I think.'

I nodded. 'Number twenty-four. We knew that. The thing is, no one in the road has been living here long enough to have known them.'

The woman nodded. 'Always moving, they are now.'

'What . . . what can you tell us about Melanie?' I asked. 'It's not my mum and dad so much as *her* we're really interested in.'

The woman smiled, a faraway look on her face. 'She was a lovely little girl, I remember that – always giggling about something or other. When she was small she used to run up here to spend her pocket money every Friday.'

'Did you know my father at all?'

The woman shook her head. 'I can just remember the look of him, but I can't recall him coming in here much.'

'And my mum?' I asked eagerly.

'Oh yes, I used to know her. Nice lady, always polite and considerate. Didn't put on airs and graces like some do with shop people.'

'I'm not sure when my family left the road,' I said slowly. 'It might have been just after I was born or it might have been before. Do you remember ... d'you remember me being born at all?'

The woman shook her head. 'I would have remembered that. Everyone made a bit of a fuss of a new baby – and they still do. They would have been in my shop for cards.'

'Do you remember Jo's Mum being pregnant, then?' Jacko asked.

She tutted, shaking her head again. 'I don't. Of course, my memory's not what it was.'

'Do you remember them moving away?'

She closed her eyes a moment. 'Now, something's come back to me. I *do* remember them moving, because there was something odd about it: they went without telling anyone, just upped and disappeared! One day they were there, the next there was a big removal van outside and they'd gone. It caused a bit of a flutter in the road, I can tell you, what with everyone speculating as to what could have happened.'

'What did people think?' I asked. One of them might have hit on the truth – whatever that was.

'Oh, we had a grand old time gossiping about them...' She looked at me: 'Sorry, dear, but you know how people like to talk. Some said your father had gone to prison, some said your mother had run off with someone else. There was even talk that the whole family had gone abroad before some big scandal broke.'

'What about Melanie?' I asked eagerly. 'Can you remember her at all then – when they moved? Did she go with them? Did she disappear at the same time?'

The woman closed her eyes again. 'If I remember

rightly, she'd already taken a job somewhere – or that was what they said. Her brow furrowed, 'It's all a long time ago; I can't really remember now. I wish my Bill was here – he'd know.'

Jacko glanced down at me. 'You see, Jo's always been told that her sister died when she was a baby. She can't remember her at all.'

The woman looked startled. 'Died! Well, I never heard that.'

'We just want to find out the truth – whether she did die ... or what.'

'I'm sure I would have heard if there had been a tragedy like that. Even if they *had* just moved.'

'There's something else,' I said. 'We think ... you see I found some of Melanie's things ... we think that she had a baby. Can you remember any gossip about her being pregnant?'

'Not a scrap! Of course, I *did* say that your family were very close-knit – I can't recall your mother mixing much with the other women round here – so it may not have got out.' She looked at me speculatively. 'Perhaps that's why she went away; she hadn't got a live-in job at all, she went away to one of those homes.' She paused. 'I can quite see your father showing her the door. I wouldn't think he'd be very tolerant about illegitimate babies!'

'That's just what we thought,' I said.

'But why can't you ask your mum all this?'

I shrugged. 'She won't answer. She gets upset – starts crying. And then my father gets annoyed and shouts and carries on at her. You see, there's always been a mystery about Melanie.'

'Well, I don't suppose I've helped you much,' the woman said. 'I'm sorry I couldn't tell you any more.'

I got up to go. 'No . . . you've been really helpful – thanks.'

She saw us through to the shop, pressed the bar of chocolate on Jacko and wouldn't take any money for it. 'If you find out, will you come back and tell me?' she asked, and we promised we would.

We set off home. It had stopped raining, thankfully, and I felt miles better – quite bright and bouncy.

'Though I don't really know why,' I said when Jacko remarked on it, 'because we haven't really found out anything new, have we? It's just the fact of finding someone who knew Melanie as a real person, I think.'

'And at least we know she didn't die when you were all living there.' He shook his head, 'What's more, I don't think she died at all.'

'Nor do I,' I said. 'I've got this really strong feeling now that she's still around.'

'Maybe she did something – got pregnant, say – and they were so horrified that they moved, did an overnight disappearance so that she couldn't find them again. Maybe she's been searching for them ever since.'

'I should think it's more likely that she was just pleased they'd gone,' I said. 'I certainly wouldn't mind if my father chucked me out and then disappeared . . . in fact I wish he would!'

The journey back was uneventful – in fact I fell asleep on Jacko's shoulder for some of the last stretch – and when we got back to our home station it was starting to get dark.

'I'd better walk you home,' Jacko said, 'unless you want to come home with me for a while first. How about it? You could meet a cornflakes dad.'

He didn't think I'd say yes, I could see that, but suddenly the thought of the next day – of a whole long, boring Sunday in that miserable house – was too awful to contemplate. I wanted today, and Jacko, to go on a bit longer.

'OK!' I said, 'you're on.'

I'd worry about being home late afterwards, I decided. Anyway, I hadn't said I'd be back at any particular time and I could always say that Mrs Salter had wanted to take us to a French restaurant to study the menu or something.

Jacko's house was modern and colourful, and his mum and dad were nice. They didn't make a big fuss of me and they didn't act like I was some creature from another planet, like my father had acted with Jacko, they just made me feel comfortable. His mum was quite stylish, too – and years younger than my mum, of course. She said that she and Jacko's father had eaten a big meal out at lunchtime so they weren't hungry, but that Jacko and I were to 'dig around in the freezer' and get ourselves whatever we wanted.

'They're really nice,' I said to Jacko when we were bent over the big chest freezer in the garage and trying to decide what to have, 'They're just how I thought they'd be.'

'Of course they're nice,' Jacko said, 'they take after me.'

I pushed him. 'It doesn't work that way round!'

Jacko was having lasagne, but I couldn't decide between that or chilli or a Chinese stir fry. They all seemed wonderfully exotic to me – Mum's idea of foreign food was a tin of spaghetti in tomato sauce.

'Hurry up!' Jacko said, 'we'll get frostbite if we hang over this freezer much longer.'

We went back into the kitchen, me clutching my chilli and rice, and started to get them ready. In the middle of it, Jacko's mum came in and said that she and his father had decided to go and see a film, so they were leaving us to it.

'There's salad in the fridge and I don't care what mess you make as long as I don't see it,' she said to Jacko.

She said goodbye and she hoped she'd see me again soon, and I wondered to myself how many girls Jacko had taken home.

'Have you told them – about me and the mystery and everything?' I asked Jacko when she'd gone.

'Of course,' he said. 'Mum's desperate to know, actually, but she's much too polite to ask in front of you. We're like that, us Jacksons – models of good behaviour . . . perfect manners.'

'If I wasn't busy stirring this chilli I'd. . .'

'Models of good behaviour, except when they find themselves alone in a house with a girl they're crazy about. . .'

He'd said he was crazy about me . . . I was just trying to take this in when he came up behind me, put his arms round me and I felt myself just melting. He turned me round and kissed me and what with one thing and another the chilli burnt in the saucepan so I never managed to actually find out what it was like. It went into the bin and I shared Jacko's lasagne.

It wasn't very late when I went home – about nine o'clock, I suppose. I felt I'd been quite rebellious enough for one day; also I didn't want Mum to be worried about me.

'Now, you're going to ask your mum to tell you

the truth, aren't you?' Jacko said sternly when we were standing at the end of my road.

I nodded.

'Tell her that it's all gone on long enough – that you want to know what *really* happened to Melanie...'

'I will,' I promised.

'You'll have to tell her the truth about today, too, tell her that you went back to Wychwood Road – that'll shake her. Say you spoke to the woman in the corner shop and kind of infer that you already know more than you do.'

'I don't want to upset her...'

'You'll have to if you want to find out the truth,' he said. 'Look, I'm sure she's a very nice woman and she can't help being like she is because she's under the influence of your dad and everything, but she's got to be made to see that not knowing – and having your father rave on at you and carry on like a tyrant for no good reason – is making you unhappy. Why should you have to suffer for whatever happened to your sister?'

'I know,' I said. 'I will try and get it out of her, I promise. It's just going to be difficult finding a time when my father isn't around.'

'Sooner or later you're going to have to confront him as well, you know. Once you've found out the truth...'

I shivered.

'Ring me. I'll be in all day tomorrow. If you can't ring for some reason, I'll see you at the bus stop on Monday. If you don't arrive, I'll be round to your house to find out what's happened to you. I'll break the door down if no one answers!'

'That should go down well with my father,' I said. I put my hand on his cheek, 'Don't worry; I'll be OK.'

'I'll be thinking about you all the time,' he said, as we parted.

Chapter 14

I stood in the kitchen, one eye on my father in the garden and the other on the white sauce I was stirring for Mum. I'd been trying to do homework all morning but had only written about four lines. I just couldn't concentrate; all I could think about was Melanie.

Eventually, from my bedroom window, I'd seen that my father was in the garden and had gone down to try and speak to Mum, making the excuse that I wanted to help her with the lunch.

'Now, don't leave that sauce, will you?' she said as I stood stirring and stirring away, 'you know you burnt it last time.'

'It's OK,' I said mechanically.

'You've only got to take your attention off it for a minute. . .' she said worriedly, as if her whole existence depended on whether or not the white sauce was perfect. It probably did, actually – considering the fuss my father made if anything was wrong with his food.

'Mum,' I said abruptly, 'you know I went out for the day yesterday?'

'Mmm,' she said. 'You didn't say much about it last night, did you? I think your father was expecting a full report.'

'If he was speaking to me he could have asked me for one himself.'

'Oh, you know what he's like, dear. He's just a bit moody, that's all.'

I pushed the saucepan off the ring a bit. 'Anyway, about yesterday...' I looked into the garden again. 'Actually, what I want to tell you is I didn't go out with Mrs Salter and the French group.'

Mum paused from preparing vegetables at the sink and looked at me blankly. 'Well, wherever did you go all day, then?' Her face suddenly took on a worried look: 'You weren't with a boy, were you?'

'Yes,' I said.

'Your father would go absolutely...'

'I know,' I said, 'but that's not all.'

She went ghostly pale and held onto the sink. 'Not ... you're not ... it couldn't happen again...'

'No, not that,' I said, realizing exactly what she was thinking. 'It's to do with her, though. It's to do with Melanie.'

Her mouth moved but she didn't say anything. I took the saucepan right off the cooker and went over to her.

'Look,' I said, taking her arm, 'I'm sorry about all this but I just *had* to know; I couldn't go on any longer not knowing the truth. I went to Wychwood Road yesterday.'

She swayed and looked so ghastly that I thought she was going to faint. I led her over to one of the kitchen chairs and sat her down in it.

'I really don't want to upset you, Mum,' I said pleadingly, 'but you must tell me the truth.'

'How did you find out – about Wychwood Road?' she asked faintly.

'I found some things of Melanie's in the loft. There were some papers with the address on. I went back there and spoke to people – the woman in the shop at the end of the road, for instance.'

'Joanna...' Mum's face was tragic, 'How could you be so deceitful? No good will come of it, you know that.'

'It wasn't *me* that was deceitful to start with – it was you and Dad.'

'No one in Wychwood Road knew anything,' she said.

'They didn't know much,' I admitted. 'The woman in the shop told me a bit, though.'

'We moved...'

'Yes, I know – overnight, without telling anyone.'

'Your father wanted it that way.'

'Look,' I said bluntly, for we seemed to be getting off the subject, 'I know something else, too: Melanie had a baby, didn't she?'

To my horror Mum looked at me and broke into hoarse, frightened sobs.

'Sssh.' I patted her arm. 'It's OK. It's not so terrible, is it? I just want to know what happened. Melanie's not dead, is she? That story you've always told me about a motorbike accident was just a lie, wasn't it?'

Mum covered her face with her hands.

'And what happened to her baby? Where *is* Susanna?'

I was frightened then that I'd gone too far because Mum just sat there, her face covered, rocking backwards and forwards in the chair and making whimpering noises.

'It'll all come out ... you'll be taken away from us,' she said indistinctly.

'What? How can I be?'

'Oh my God ... I knew this would happen,' she

whispered. 'I told him all along that we should have told the truth...'

'What *is* the truth?' I asked fiercely, shaking her arm. 'You've got to tell me!'

But she couldn't, or wouldn't, and I was frightened to press her in case she went hysterical or collapsed or something. She just sat there for what seemed like ages, not speaking, looking at me every now and again and rocking. In the end I was so scared that my father would come in and find her like this that I asked her if she wanted to go and lie down, and when she nodded slightly, led her upstairs and into her bedroom. She didn't come out for the rest of the afternoon so I cooked the lunch on my own and told Dad that she had a migraine. At teatime she appeared again, pale but composed, and got the tea ready as if nothing had happened.

I felt unbearably frustrated. I tried to ring Jacko and tell him what had happened but I just couldn't manage to get on my own to make a call.

I didn't sleep much; I felt so mixed up. One part of me was blissfully happy because of the things Jacko had said the day before, the other part of me was in conflict, full of 'but what ifs' and 'but hows?'

In the morning I waited until my father had gone to work as usual, and then I went down to breakfast. Mum was perhaps a little quieter than normal, but otherwise showed no sign of still being upset by what I'd said the previous day.

'Home at normal time, dear?' she asked as I left.

I nodded. 'Are you out, then? It's not your usual afternoon for the Oxfam shop, is it?'

'It isn't, but I thought I might ask if I can do an extra few sessions. It'll get me out of the house.'

'Good idea,' I said. 'Why don't you go out to work properly, though? You could easily get shop work round here.'

'No, your father wouldn't like it,' she said, and turned away before I could say anything else.

I fastened on my cloak and ran towards the bus stop. Jacko saw me, stepped out of line and came to the back of the queue with me.

'Well?' he demanded. 'You might have rung me up. I've been perched by the phone all weekend.'

'Nothing.' I said, shaking my head. 'She clammed up. Got nearly hysterical. I . . . felt so sorry for her that I had to stop asking.'

'Oh, Jo. . .'

'She said. . .' I hesitated, wondering, 'She said something about me being taken away. .''No good will come of it; you'll be taken away from us" she said.'

Jacko looked puzzled, frowning deeply. A crowded bus came along and I made a move towards it but Jacko held back.

'Let it go,' he said, 'I'm just trying to work something out.'

I took his hand. 'What?' I asked, but he didn't say anything, just squeezed my fingers.

As everyone else got on the bus his face suddenly cleared. 'I know what happened,' he said simply. 'I know exactly.'

'What?' I stared at him, gripped his hand. 'What d'you know? How can you just have found something out while we were standing here?'

'It just all became clear.'

I shook his arm impatiently. 'Come *on!* What're you talking about? Tell me!'

He shook his head. 'I think your mother should tell you. I'm going to go back with you now and confront her.'

'We can't!'

'We can.' He started walking away from the bus stop, very fast, and I had no alternative but to run after him.

'I don't want to . . . she won't tell us,' I said breathlessly. 'She'll go mad if you ask. I mean, she doesn't even know about you and if you suddenly turn up and start questioning her about Melanie – about her dead daughter – I mean, she'll probably. . .'

'Not dead,' Jacko interrupted. 'Definitely not dead.'

I followed him down the road, my mind churning and my stomach matching it.

I didn't use my key, I rang the doorbell and Mum answered straight away.

'Did you forget. . .' she began, and then her eyes slid past me to Jacko.

'This is Jacko, Mum,' I said.

Jacko held out his hand. 'Hello, Mrs McIver,' he said, and after a moment my mother took his hand and shook it timidly, looking at me all the time.

'Can we come in, then?' I said, because she was still standing across the doorway. She moved back slightly. 'I want . . . we both want to speak to you.'

We went in, she closed the door and we stood in a nervous semi-circle in the hall, just looking at each other.

'Mrs McIver, I just wanted to tell you that I know the secret about Joanna,' Jacko said. He looked at Mum and he nodded slightly, meaningfully, as if to say that the game was up and she might as well come clean. 'I'll tell her the truth myself if you like, but I just thought it might be better coming from you.'

There was a long, long silence. Mum swayed slightly, went pale, but otherwise showed no sign of distress. She took my hand in her own. 'Ah, Joanna...' she said, looking at me tenderly.

I felt dream-like, removed... as if I was acting a part but someone had forgotten to tell me what character I was playing.

'I was going to tell you... I'd made up my mind you'd have to know.'

'What?' I whispered.

She smiled slightly. 'That you're not really mine. You are Melanie's child. My granddaughter.'

The silence went on for ages this time as I stared at Mum – or the person I'd always thought of as Mum – completely stunned, and then she and I both started crying and Jacko disappeared somewhere.

We cried for a while and then, arms round each other, we sat down on the stairs. I felt completely exhausted, as if I'd come to the end of a long, long race. I wasn't theirs, I was Melanie's. But of course ... of course. It was a bombshell, an utter shock – and yet it was so obvious. All the clues had been there, and the sense of not fitting, not really belonging to them, but I hadn't been able to read the signs. Somewhere, though, deep in my heart, I felt as if I'd known the truth all along.

'Melanie found out she was having a baby when she was sixteen,' Mum said after a while. 'For weeks ... months ... we were frightened to tell your father, but he eventually found out for himself.'

'What happened?' I asked.

'You can guess – he read her the riot act, wouldn't

have anything to do with her. He threw her out the very night he found out, wouldn't even let her take her things.'

I shook my head wonderingly, thinking of the photographs upstairs of lovely, happy Melanie.

'Oh, he was wicked...'

'Why did you let him do it, then?'

'I had no choice. I tried but there was nothing I could do.'

'What happened to Melanie?'

'She went into a local authority home. She contacted me and I used to go and visit her in the afternoons. She had the baby...' Mum squeezed my shoulder, 'she had you, and you were supposed to go for adoption. She couldn't have kept you, you see — she was still at school.'

'What about my... my father, my real father?'

'His name was Sam. He was a nice lad, but he was at school, too, and his parents were desperate to get him away. They took him abroad somewhere to finish his education.'

'And then what happened to Melanie?'

'Well, when it came to giving you up to your adoptive parents, we just couldn't do it. Mel and I... we cried and cried all one day, and in the end I just decided I'd have to take you back home with me. You see, I knew he'd never have Mel home again — so I'd lost *her*, but I couldn't bear to lose you as well.'

'But what on earth did... did my father say?'

Mum sighed. 'Oh, he didn't speak to me for months. I'd made up my mind I was going to keep you, though, and he knew that if he wanted me to stay, he'd have to have you as well.'

'And what about Melanie?'

'Oh – he kept his word; he wouldn't have her in the house. He let me keep the baby – he let me keep you – as long as she gave up all rights and never came near us again. She called you Susanna but we renamed you, and that was when we moved – just after you were born. You never went to live in Wychwood Road.'

'And then you came here with a new baby and everyone thought it was yours...'

She nodded.

'But why did you have to pretend Melanie was dead?' I clutched at her suddenly, 'She's not dead, is she?'

Mum shook her head. 'No, she's not dead. That was your father again. He wanted you brought up as our own child and said that every trace of Melanie should disappear and she should never be spoken of. He said that if people found out that you weren't ours you'd be taken away. That's why we couldn't let you have a passport – you'd have needed a birth certificate for that and yours would have Melanie's name on as your mother.'

'But sooner or later I'd have had to know...'

'That's what I kept saying. He wouldn't listen to me, though, and you know what he's like for getting his own way.'

I rested my head on Mum's shoulder. 'Where is she now?' I asked.

'Scotland, the last I heard. She used to ring me up but once your father was in and answered the phone and she's never called since.'

We were silent for a moment and then Jacko put his head round the kitchen door.

'Tea?' he asked.

I stared at him. 'I'd forgotten you were here!'

He smiled quizzically. 'I thought I'd leave you alone for a while.'

Mum and I got up from the stairs, I blew my nose on a handkerchief she handed me and then we went into the kitchen.

'What will you do now?' she asked. 'Will you try and find her?'

I shook my head. 'I will ... eventually. It's all too much at the moment, though. I can't take it in properly.'

'I know she'd love to see you...' Mum's eyes filled with tears again, 'but I don't want to lose you either.'

I hugged her. 'You won't! I'm going to tell my father – *my grandfather* – that I know, though, and I'm going to get my own passport now, and do a few other things I've always wanted to do. I'm going to make some changes; start living a little bit.'

'This tea is getting stewed,' Jacko said plaintively, so we sat down at the table and he poured out two cups. He'd made it in the coffee pot instead of the tea pot, but I wasn't going to tell him.

'This reminds me of when Mel used to bring Sam home,' Mum said. 'We used to have some good laughs, we did.'

Jacko grinned. 'We'll see if we can't turn the clock back then,' he said, 'We're good at making mums laugh, us Jacksons.'

I smiled at him and realized that all the cloudiness had gone out of my life. It had turned itself upside down: I had a new mum I hadn't known about and a gran and grandad, but in spite of all this upheaval and turmoil I still had Jacko. The need to belong to someone, the longing to be loved – all that was fulfilled in Jacko. Whatever happened from now on was a bonus...

heartlines

Where true love comes first

Other books in the series for you to enjoy

Mary Hooper
Love Emma £1.25

Emma begins her nursing training with high hopes. Determined to achieve something for herself, she still finds the three-year separation from her established world of family and friends a little frightening. In letters to her parents, best friend and boyfriend – and in entries in her secret diary – Emma describes her new world in warm and witty detail . . . hard-working, occasionally exciting and always exhausting – but there are rewards; *and* a student doctor named Luke . . .

Jill Young
Three Summers On £1.25

For three years Nell had depended almost entirely on Mark, her good-looking young social worker. When she found out that he was moving away, she felt bitter, betrayed and all alone. But during the summer, at a holiday centre for handicapped kids, she realized there were those much worse off than herself. She formed the first important friendship of her life with Marion, and although her romance with Marion's wild, cocky brother Dan came to nothing, there was still Jim to turn to. Suddenly the future looked good ...

Jane Butterworth
Spotlight on Sam £1.25

Sam was always putting herself down. She was too tall, her nose too long, her feet too big, and she wasn't much good at anything. Things look better though, when her natural talent for the stage lands her with a part – and a date from Tom, the dishy assistant stage manager.

Wild in the Country £1.25

Jo had gloomily resigned herself to working full-time on her father's farm now that he'd insisted she leave school without trying for university. Even worse, she half-believed she would end up marrying Davy Morrison, the boy from the next farm she'd known all her life, just to please her old-fashioned father.

Then into her life came Nic Daniell. He was tall, blond and good-looking, and his almost arrogant self-confidence was in direct contrast to Davy's country boy awkwardness. Suddenly Jo felt that maybe things would turn out better than she'd ever hoped . . .

Anthea Cohen
Dangerous Love £1.25

Sandra isn't a dare-devil like her friend Edie, but she longs for the excitement of being with a wild crowd like Dan and his friends. During their quiet 'Sandra nights' she comes to know a different, more sensitive, Dan – yet there are still 'Dan nights' when he wants her to join in the excitement of the crowd and their dangerous schemes...

Anita Eires
Teacher's Pet £1.25

It should have been so simple – but life is never that simple, and certainly not for Amanda, for the grey-eyed, handsome and exciting man she loves just happens to be her English teacher. Amanda is convinced that Harry's interest in her is based on more than her literary talents – why else had he chosen her especially to work with him on the school magazine?

Ann de Gale
Island Encounter £1.50

Above all, Nic was a rebel. She rebelled against her schoolmates' endless hunt for boyfriends – and she tried to rebel when her charming, but irresponsible, father offered to take her on a camping holiday in Corfu ... for single parents and their children. A ridiculous idea, she thought, and downright unfair to the rest of her family.

In spite of her reluctance. Nic went to Corfu – and soon she was falling under the spell of the gnarled olive trees, the silent craggy rocks and the beautiful, translucent sea.

But she also fell under the spell of a solemn Scots boy she nicknamed 'Hamish' – whose real name was Jon ...

John Harvey
Wild Love £1.25

Helping her divorced father run an arts centre in the wild Yorkshire moors didn't at first appeal to Jane, but the photographer in her was soon caught up in the rugged beauty of Emily Brontë's world, while the romantic in her was at once captivated by Gareth, whose black eyes blazed with an anger both frightening and strangely attractive.

But with the arrival of blond, blue-eyed poet Martin McCabe, the fantasy of *Wuthering Heights* began to turn into reality and Jane found herself wondering to what lengths Gareth's jealousy would drive him . . .

All Pan books are available at your local bookshop or newsagent, or can be ordered direct from the publisher. Indicate the number of copies required and fill in the form below.

Send to: **CS Department, Pan Books Ltd., P.O. Box 40, Basingstoke, Hants. RG21 2YT.**

or phone: 0256 469551 (Ansaphone), quoting title, author and Credit Card number.

Please enclose a remittance* to the value of the cover price plus: 60p for the first book plus 30p per copy for each additional book ordered to a maximum charge of £2.40 to cover postage and packing.

*Payment may be made in sterling by UK personal cheque, postal order, sterling draft or international money order, made payable to Pan Books Ltd.

Alternatively by Barclaycard/Access:

Card No. ☐☐☐☐☐☐☐☐☐☐☐☐☐☐☐☐

———————————————————————————————
Signature:

Applicable only in the UK and Republic of Ireland.

While every effort is made to keep prices low, it is sometimes necessary to increase prices at short notice. Pan Books reserve the right to show on covers and charge new retail prices which may differ from those advertised in the text or elsewhere.

NAME AND ADDRESS IN BLOCK LETTERS PLEASE:

....

Name ——————————————————————————

Address ——————————————————————————

——————————————————————————————

——————————————————————————————

——————————————————————————————

3/87